creative Handcrafts

Grades 4, 5, 6 (Juniors)

112 Handcrafts for
Church • School • VBS • Home
8 pages of Recipes and Hints

Compiled by Eleanor L. Doan

G/L
REGAL
BOOKS

A Division of G/L Publications
Glendale, California, U.S.A.

HO. ˅

745

ACKNOWLEDGMENT

The handcrafts included in this book are taken from the *Handcraft Encyclopedia* by the same author. They are assembled here for greater convenience in use with children in grades 4,5 and 6.

Published by
Regal Books Division, G/L Publications
Glendale, California 91209, U.S.A.
Library of Congress Catalog No.: 72-93601
ISBN: 0-8307-0210-5

CONTENTS

SAND CASTING

Materials: Clean sand; patching plaster; small, pretty stones or shells; old costume jewelry, marbles, pieces of colored glass; water; 6" piece of heavy cord; poster paints; brush. (Note: If you do not have access to a sandy area, pour 2 bags of sand in a large flat box.)

Procedure: Moisten sand so that it is damp for a depth of several inches. With both hands, make a mold for the object desired by scooping away sand and pressing designs in sand until you have the proper shape (sketch a). Press into place the decorations: marbles, costume jewelry, colored glass, etc. (sketch b).

Mix the patching plaster to a thick consistency. Pour plaster into mold (sketch c). Knot 6" cord at each end and insert into plaster to form hanging loop (sketch d). Be sure to press cord at least 1" into plaster. Allow plaster to harden for 30 minutes (longer if weather is damp). Remove plaster from mold and brush off excess sand. Paint with poster colors (sketch e).

Time required to make: 1 to 1½ hours plus drying time

1

GARDEN TOOL CARRIER

Materials: 4 fruit lug ends, 1 yd. clothesline rope, awl, saw, sandpaper, paint and brush, hammer and nails, adhesive tape

Procedure: Remove all nails from lug ends. In two of the lug ends bore two holes. Holes should be 1″ in from one side and 5″ apart (sketch a). Nail these pieces upright to another lug end (sketch b). Measure width of ends for tool carrier and cut these from the fourth lug end, discarding leftover piece (sketch c). Nail ends to carrier. Sand and paint the tool case. To make handles, cut rope in half; make a tight knot in one end of each piece and slip opposite end through a hole in one side of the tool carrier so knot is on inside (sketch d), then through hole on opposite side as shown in sketch e. Tie knots so rope will not slip through holes. Tape handles together in center as shown in sketch f. Carrier is ready to use.

Time required to make: 2 to 3 hours

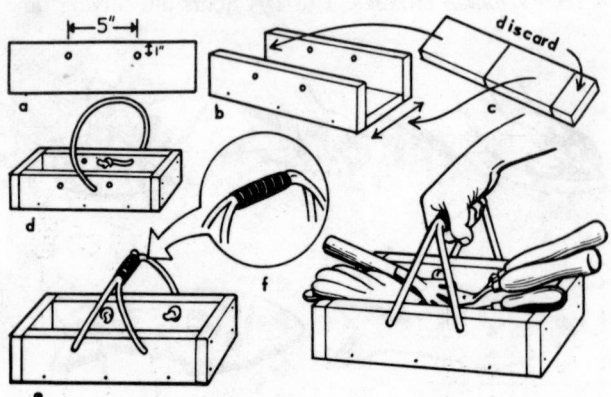

NOTE BOARD HOLDER

Materials: Heavy cardboard, such as a grocery carton, 18" x 10"; a 7" x 10" piece of lightweight cardboard (suit box); pencil; wrapping paper; poster paints; brush; curtain ring; adhesive tape; glue or staple gun; razor blade in holder or an X-acto knife

Procedure: Draw a pattern of a sailor on wrapping paper by following sketch a. Trace on heavy cardboard. Cut out sailor with a razor blade or X-acto knife.

Paint the sailor with poster paints. Make his face and hands flesh colored, his hat white, his tie and shoes black and his suit blue.

Cut a 7" x 10" note holder board from a suit box. Draw 6 right-angle arrows (each side of angle is 1") on the board and cut along lines (sketch b). Carefully glue or staple edges of note holder to sailor making sure openings are not sealed in the process. Draw and paint sailor's hands on note board to match those on heavy cardboard (sketch c).

Attach a curtain ring to the back of the sailor with a piece of adhesive tape and hang on wall.

Time required to make: 1 to 2 hours

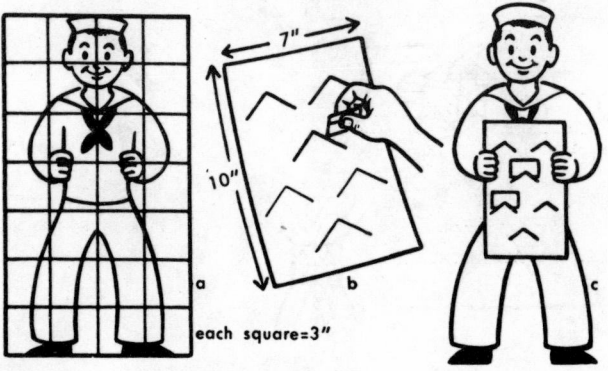

each square = 3"

3

NECKERCHIEF SLIDE

Materials: Nut of suitable size for slide (such as a horse chestnut) or piece of bamboo from old fishing pole, small drill and vise, sandpaper, paint, shellac or clear fingernail polish, paintbrush

Procedure: Saw bamboo into 1½" pieces. If a nut is used, bore out center and clean out nut meats. To hold nut firmly, place in small vise when using drill.

Sandpaper edges and inside of bamboo to insure smooth sliding. Roll sandpaper around a pencil to work inside the slide. Paint a design on slide. When dry, coat with shellac or clear fingernail polish.

Time required to make: 45 minutes, plus drying time

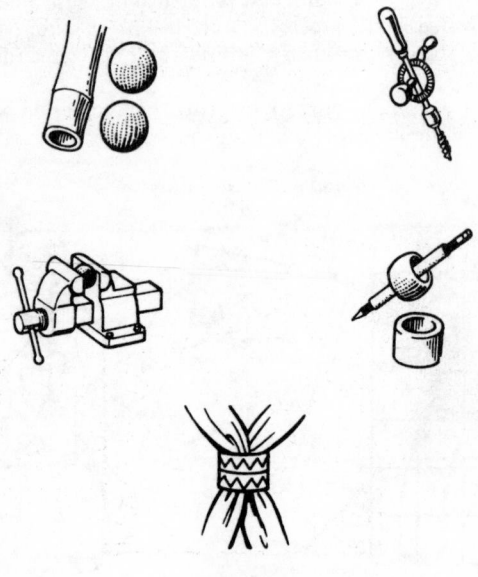

METAL BLOTTER CORNERS

Materials: 1 small can per corner, tin snips, compression can opener, Scotch tape, nail, hammer, felt scraps, block of wood, glue

Procedure: Remove label from can before washing. Cut off top and bottom just below lip of can with compression can opener or tin snips. Cut down side seam and flatten can. Have tin twice as long as the width. Measure and cut tin to desired size and bind with Scotch tape. Scratch line down center (on wrong side) forming two squares. Scratch lines from one end of center line to opposite corners. Decorate large central triangle by stippling with nail and hammer on wrong side (initials may be used). (Place tin on block of wood when stippling.) When design is finished, fold tin on diagonal lines so that sides meet at center to form a triangle. (Fold over table edge.) Tap lightly with hammer to smooth folds. Cut piece of felt slightly smaller than triangle and glue to back of corner. Make four to form set and slip on colored desk blotter.

Time required to make: 45 minutes to 1 hour

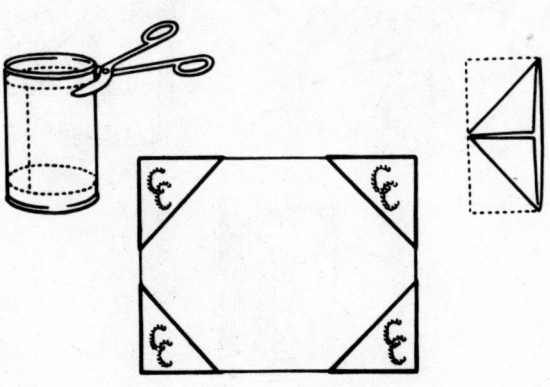

SCONCE OR CANDLESTICK

Materials: 1 No. 2½-size tin can with top removed, Scotch tape, medium-size nail, 1 bottle cap, ½" paper fastener, candle, hammer, file, tin snips

Procedure: Remove and save label. Wash can. Punch hole in center of closed end of can with nail. Use tin snips and cut down ½" from both sides of seam of can to rim of closed end. Leave this strip attached for handle. Fold label in half, lengthwise, blank side out. Draw pattern for sconce and cut out. Wrap paper around can and hold in place with Scotch tape. Mark outline on can with a nail and cut along line with tin snips. Remove pattern. Smooth edges with a file, especially handle strip. Roll strip down and under. Punch hole in top back of sconce for hanging. Punch hole in center of bottle cap. Fasten bottle cap to inside bottom of can with ½" paper fastener (inserted from outside). Put candle in bottle cap holder.

Time required to make: 1½ to 2 hours

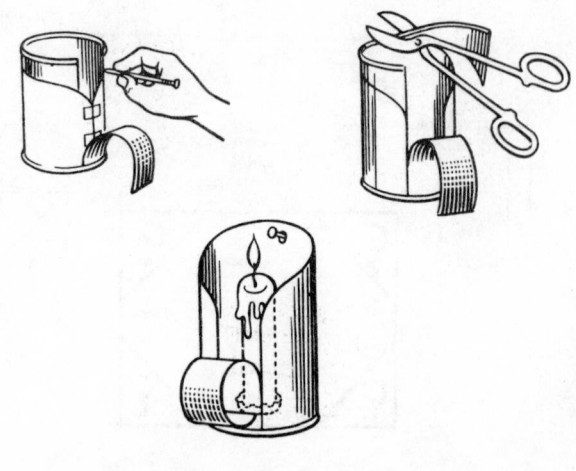

BARREL PLANTER OR PENCIL HOLDER

Materials: 1 squat peanut can, 13 medium-size clip clothespins, soft copper wire, pliers, brown stain or shellac, brush, 2 rubber bands

Procedure: Remove springs from clothespins. To do this, hold clothespin with both hands (see sketch a) and twist apart. Place clothespin halves around can, with outside part against can (sketch b). (Use rubber bands to hold clothespins in place.) Wrap two strands of copper wire around clothespins, fitting one into top groove and one into bottom groove. Twist wire tightly with pliers to hold clothespins firmly in place. Stain or shellac barrel. When dry, fill barrel with dirt and add a plant. Or, use container as a pencil or trinket holder.

Time required to make: About 1 hour

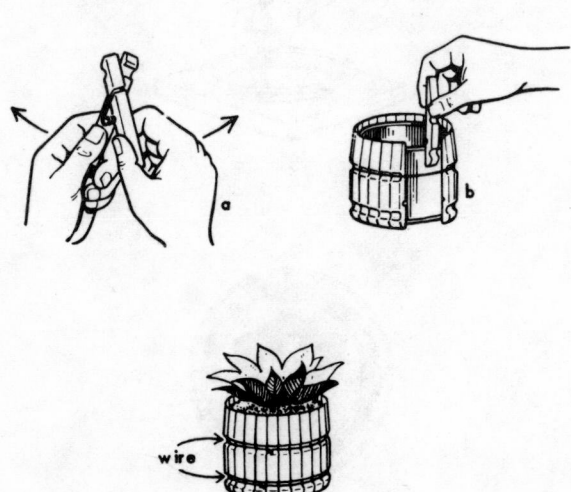

7

TIN CREST

Materials: Large plain pie tin, blunt nail, hammer, block of wood larger than pie tin, enamel, brush

Procedure: Scratch crest or coat of arms on inside of tin with nail. Place tin on block of wood and stipple design with blunt nail and hammer. Work from inside of tin. Design will stand out on back. Paint with enamel. Punch hole in top of rim for hanging.

Time required to make: 45 minutes to 1 hour

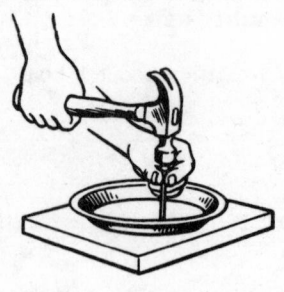

CROSS PUZZLE

Materials: Piece of plywood 9"x11", small saw, sand-paper, paper, carbon paper, pencil, ruler, varnish and brush, small box

Procedure: Enlarge pattern (sketch a) and trace on plywood. Cut out carefully along lines traced on cross (sketch b). Discard pieces which are not a part of the puzzle (or use for small plaques). Sand edges carefully. Varnish both sides of the five pieces. Place in a small box. See if your friends can put puzzle together.

Time required to make: About 1 hour

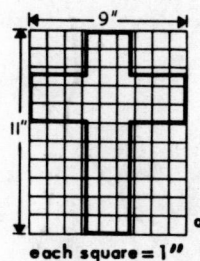

each square = 1"

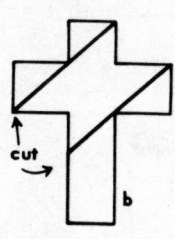

cut

SEA MONSTER PUPPET

Materials: 1 man's sock; piece of wrapping paper; piece of red cloth 4" x 16"; cardboard (same size as cloth) from cereal box; scissors; ruler; pencil; needle; thread; 3 buttons (2 green and 1 red); ½ yd. narrow fringe; 2 gummed reinforcements

Procedure: Cut sock as shown in sketch a by dotted line. Measure length of cut and width of foot piece. From these dimensions draw a mouth piece on wrapping paper, making it double (sketch b). Use this as pattern to cut mouth piece from cardboard and red cloth. Turn sock inside out and sew red material to sock with an overhand stitch (see sketch c). Turn sock right side out and insert cardboard. Sew fringe across top of head and loop it on each side for ears. Sew on green buttons for eyes and red button for nose. Paste gummed reinforcements on button eyes. Place hand in head with thumb in lower jaw (see sketch d).

Time required to make: 1 to 1½ hours

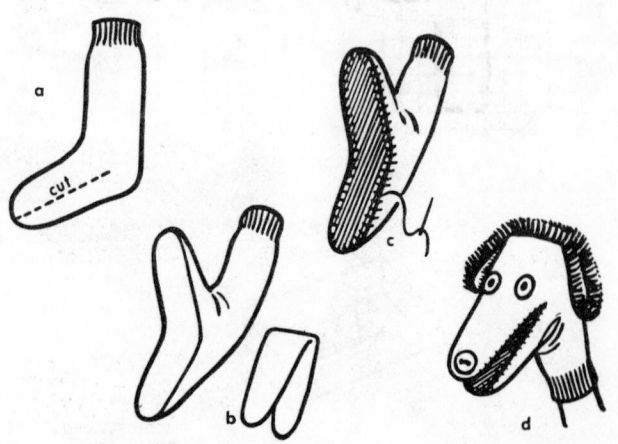

JEWELRY BOX

Materials: 1 egg carton (type shown in sketch); lid from another carton; rubber-base paint in color you desire; brush; strip of cloth 2″ wide and 3 times length around carton; pinking shears; sewing materials; shells or imitation jewels, glue

Procedure: Paint carton inside and out and allow to dry. Also paint outside of extra lid (sketches a, b). Trim one edge of cloth with pinking shears (sketch c). Sew ends together. Gather smooth edge to fit around edge of extra lid. Sew, or glue, ruffling to this lid (sketches d and e). Set bottom of the hinged box inside the separate top (sketch f) and glue. Decorate top of jewelry box by gluing on jewels or shells (sketch g).

Time required to make: 1½ to 2 hours

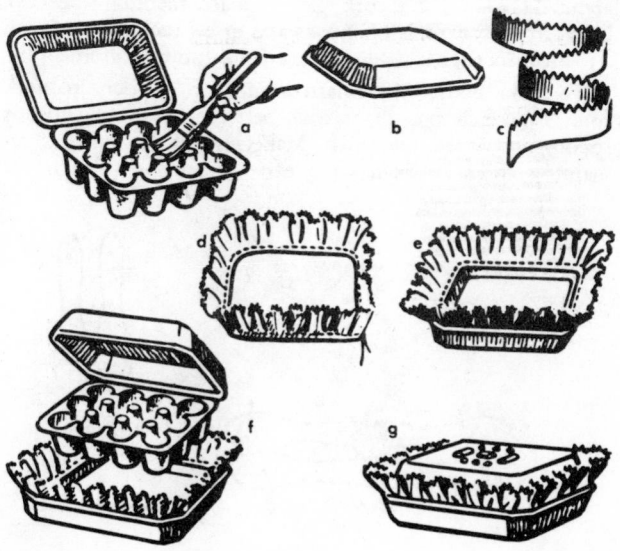

11

MAUDE THE MULE

Materials: 8 small 3" wooden spoons like those used with ice cream cups; 5 round toothpicks; 1 cork 1" in diameter; 4 corks ¾" in diameter and 1" to 1¼" long; 5 very small corks (¼" to ⅜" diameter) or 1 large cork from which 10 smaller pieces ¼" thick can be cut; 2 red thumbtacks; 2 gummed reinforcements; 1" square black construction paper; 3½" length of black fringe; 1 pin; ½ yd. black yarn; knife; small drill; glue

Procedure: Drill carefully (to avoid splitting) a hole in both ends of each spoon: ½" from wide end and ⅜" from handle end.

To make head and neck of mule, push a toothpick through large end of largest cork, then attach a spoon (wide end) on each side. Cut smallest corks in half (or cut small pieces from large cork) and fasten a piece on each end of toothpick. Cut off toothpicks so they extend about 1/16" beyond cork pieces. Place medium-size cork between narrow ends of spoons and insert toothpick (sketch a). Push toothpick through cork from top to bottom.

To make body, attach narrow ends of 2 spoons to neck spoons (sketch b). Place cork between opposite ends of spoons and insert toothpick. Make legs by fastening 2 remaining corks between wide ends of spoons (sketch c).

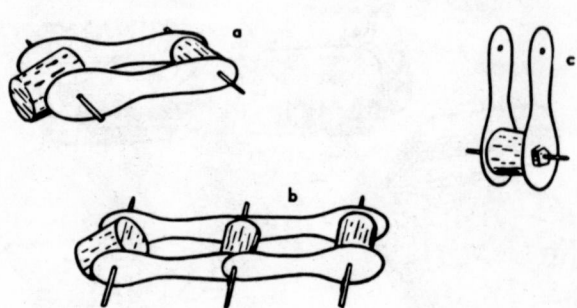

12

Add small cork pieces and trim toothpicks as when making head. Attach legs to body (sketch d), adding cork washers and trimming off toothpicks.

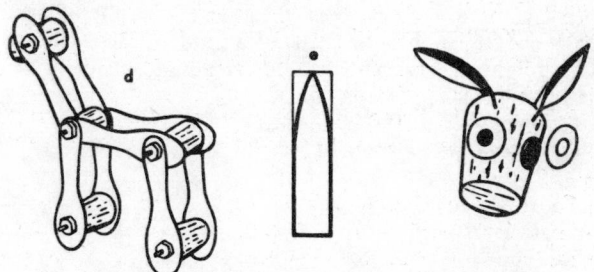

Fasten the red thumbtacks in head cork for eyes and paste a gummed reinforcement over each. Cut 2 slits in cork above eyes and insert ears cut from pattern given in sketch e. Cut yarn in 4" lengths and loop over cork for tail (sketch f). Attach piece of fringe to head with pin, then glue other end to shoulder cork. If necessary, trim fringe for suitable mane.

Time required to make: 1 to 1½ hours

13

PAPER BAG LANTERN

Materials: One medium-size paper bag, flashlight, crayons, scissors

Procedure: Draw a face on paper bag with mouth near open end of bag. Draw eyes, then cut out pupils of eyes. Shake out bag so it is the shape of a head and tie bulb end of flashlight in bag, with handle extending outside. Flash the light to make the eyes blink.

Time required to make: 15 to 20 minutes

MACARONI PLAQUE

Materials: Piece of plywood, size depending upon poem, proverb or Bible verse chosen; sandpaper; macaroni alphabet letters; stain; shellac; paintbrushes; glue; water colors and brush; gold cord or rickrack

Procedure: Carefully sandpaper plywood, then stain to desired shade. When dry, glue on macaroni letters to spell the proverb, Bible verse or poem, etc., chosen. If you wish, paint the letters any color desired. Decorate, then shellac entire plaque. If this plaque is to be a gift to a family, this poem is appropriate:

> Bless this house
> Oh Lord we pray.
> Make it safe
> By night and day.

Time required to make: 1½ to 2½ hours

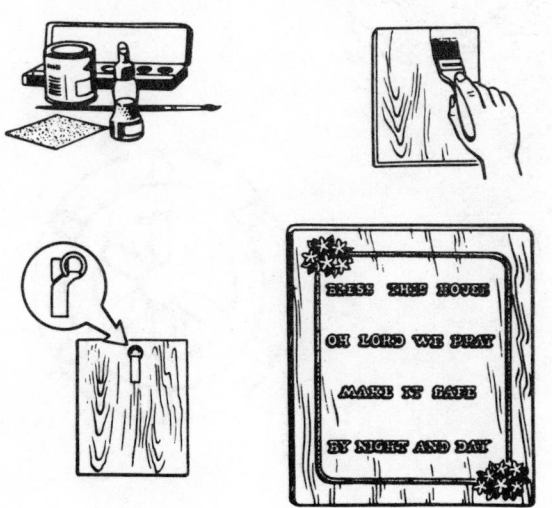

15

COASTER

Materials: Thin sheet of cork large enough to fit under a glass, scissors, poster paint, paint brush, pencil, shellac

Procedure: Trace desired pattern on cork and cut out. Paint design on top of coaster and shellac.

Time required to make: 30 minutes

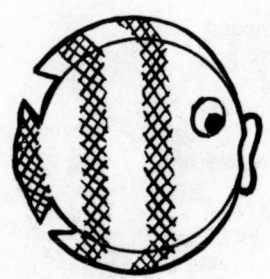

RECORD INDIAN BOWL

Materials: 1 old phonograph record (78), 1 stick or knife, enough plastic wood or putty to fill hole, enamel, paint brush, pan of hot water, newspaper

Procedure: Place record in hot water. When it begins to soften, remove with knife or stick. Place on newspaper and begin shaping. Work quickly as records dry fast. If bowl becomes too hard, dip in hot water. Fill hole with plastic wood or putty. Enamel an Indian design and let dry.

Time required to make: 30 to 60 minutes

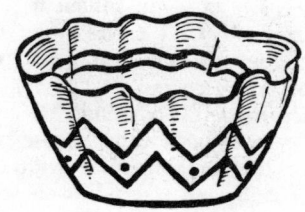

MULTICOLORED BOTTLES AND JARS

Materials: Bottles or jars of attractive shapes; colored paper (from magazines, comic books, envelope linings, drawing paper, etc.); scissors; glue; clear shellac and brush, or clear plastic spray

Procedure: Select an attractively shaped jar or bottle (with large opening). Cut colored paper in small pieces in several sizes and shapes such as triangles, circles, rectangles. Or, use one consistent shape, but be sure to vary size.

Glue cut paper on jar piece by piece, overlapping each piece so all the surface (except the bottom) is covered. Allow to dry. If papers are closely blended in color, you may paste a dark silhouette design over the cut-paper background. Give entire vase two coats of shellac or clear plastic finish from a spray can. (Do not hold plastic spray too close to container.) Use containers as vases, planters, pencil holders, book ends.

To make book ends, choose two identical jars with lids. Paint lids to harmonize with containers. Fill containers with sand, and screw lids on securely.

Time required to make: 2 hours

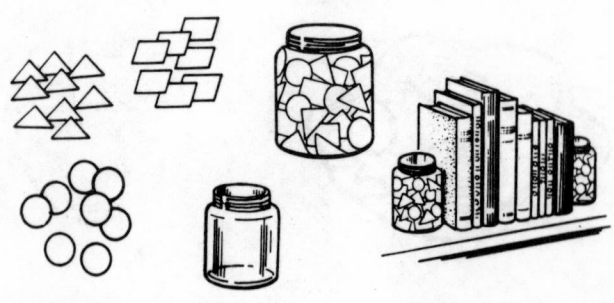

WHALE SPINDLE

Materials: Mixing bowl; large spoon; patching plaster; cardboard; water; 4" nail; 2 jewels or small pieces of colored glass; felt; scissors; paint; paintbrush; glue; wax paper

Procédure: Cut a piece of cardboard the shape of a whale's tail (sketch a). Mix just enough water with 1½ cups of plaster to make a stiff mixture for modeling. Work on wax paper. Begin at once to shape the tail of the whale from the plaster. To help in doing this, build plaster around the cardboard tail. Keep working the plaster and shape the body carefully until you have desired effect (sketch b). Put the nail, head down, into the back of the whale before the plaster becomes too hard. Also insert jewels or colored glass into plaster for eyes. Let object harden for at least 45 minutes. Then paint any color you wish. Cut a piece of felt to fit bottom of whale and glue on. This will be a useful spindle on any desk, for kitchen lists or family reminders (sketch c).

Time required to make: 1 hour plus drying time

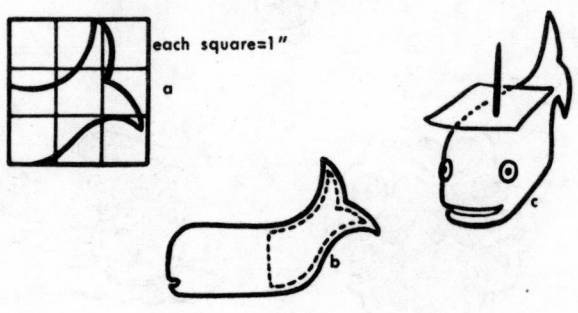

BOTTLE CAP CRAFT

Hot Dish Mat

Materials: Piece of sturdy material 12"x15"; 19 bottle caps; 6" squares of cardboard, felt or cork; needle and thread

Procedure: Cut 19 circles 3" in diameter from material. Baste thread around circumference of circle, place cap in center, smooth side down, and draw thread tight. Fasten thread securely. Arrange covered caps (smooth side up) on cardboard in 2 circles around a center cap. Sew caps to cardboard. Draw around caps and trim off cardboard edges. Trace on second piece of cardboard (felt or cork) and glue 2 pieces together.

Time required to make: 1 to 1½ hours

Foot Scraper

Materials: 1 block of wood (end of orange crate); 107 nails ⅝" long with large heads, or extra long tacks; 95 bottle caps, ball peen hammer, 2 large nails, square of rubber tubing size of block

Procedure: Remove corks from bottle caps with large nail. Place caps on block, top down so edges are up, in alternate rows of 10 and 9 caps. Start hole in center of each cap with large nail and hammer. Remove nail and press ⅝" nail or tack into hole. Hammer with ball peen hammer. When all caps are nailed to board, tack rubber on back.

Time required to make: About 2 hours

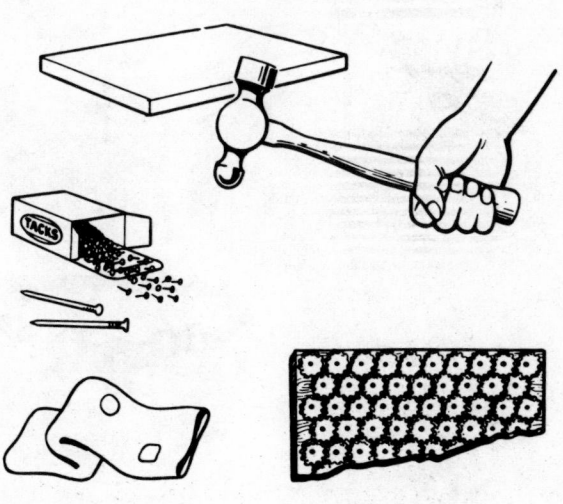

Belt

Materials: Nail, hammer, 16 to 20 bottle caps, 10- or 12-ft. heavy white cord, adhesive tape

Procedure: Punch 4 holes in top of bottle caps. Remove cork. Cut cord in half. Tightly bind all ends of cord with tape to make stringing of caps easier. String caps on cord, using both pieces, in cross-stitch fashion. Cross is formed on inside of cap. Leave about 1" between caps (measuring on top of cap). Adjust belt to fit waist. Leave equal lengths of cord at each end for tying.

Time required to make: 45 minutes to 1 hour

CHEF NOTE PAD

Materials: Piece of white cardboard 3½" x 8", scissors, pencil, piece of tracing paper, crayons, 1 small pad of paper, one 10" piece of string, 1 small pencil, paste (substitute sandpaper for pad of paper if you make a match scratcher)

Procedure: Enlarge and trace chef pattern in sketch a on a white cardboard. Cut out and let child color one. Help children paste note pad in place. Tie one end of string to pencil, make loop by tying other end of string about 1" above pencil (sketch b). Slip loop over head and draw up tightly. Here is a handy note pad.

Time required to make: 30 to 60 minutes

PET'S BED

Materials: An apple box or similar wood box; paper; pencil; scissors; nails; hammer; sandpaper; paint; paintbrush; coping saw and small hand saw

Procedure: Carefully take the box apart, removing the nails. Enlarge a pattern from sketch a (or draw a picture of your own pet) on paper for the ends of the bed. Measure to make sure you can cut the 2 ends from the ends of the boxes. Cut out pet pattern from paper and trace on box ends. Cut out the ends of bed with saw and sandpaper carefully.

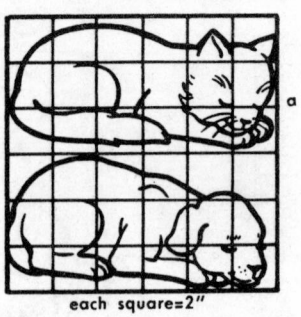

each square=2"

The bottom of the bed should measure 19" x 11". (If your pet is large, make bed bigger.) The back of the bed should measure 19" x 6¼". Cut these pieces out with a hand saw. Also cut 3 pieces 11" x 1¾" from box ends. Sandpaper.

Nail two 11" x 1¾" strips to 1 side of the 19" x 11" piece, one about 2" from each end of board. Nail the

24

third piece in the center of the board. This forms the
bottom of the pet's bed (sketch b.) Now nail the 19"x6¼"

piece at a right angle to the bed bottom. Notice sketch c
so you will nail the back correctly. Now you are ready
to nail the ends on the bed. Be sure to measure carefully
so both ends are in the same position.

Paint bed. If you wish, paint ends the same color as
your pet. Decorate with paint or wood-burning set.

Time required to make: 3 hours

LOG BOOK

Materials: 2 pieces of ¼" plywood 9" x 12"; small saw; hand drill; ruler; pencil; paint or stain; paintbrush; old leather wallet, glove or belt (for hinges); scissors; 24 colored thumbtacks; sandpaper; 1 shoelace or leather thong for tying book together; paper for inside of book; paper punch; wood-burning pen

Procedure: Cut 2 pieces of plywood exactly the same size for the covers. For the front, mark and saw a 1¼" strip lengthwise from one piece of plywood (sketch a). This narrow strip is to help hold the book together and form a hinged cover. Drill 3 holes in the 1¼" strip, one 2½" from each end and one in the center. Be sure these holes are in the center, widthwise. Drill matching holes in the back cover of the book (sketch a). Carefully sandpaper the covers, especially at the corners. Draw and woodburn an appropriate design on cover. Then stain or paint and allow to dry.

Cut 3 leather pieces 1" x 2". Thumbtack these hinges onto the front cover to connect the 1¼" wood strip and the 8" x 12" piece of wood. Put 4 thumbtacks on each end of the leather hinge as shown in sketch b. Two of these

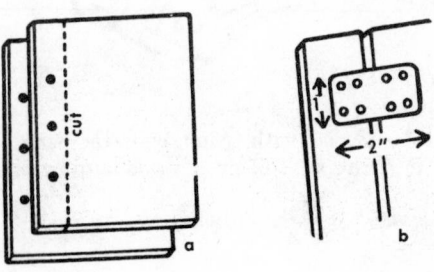

hinges should be ½″ from top and bottom of book. The third should be in the center. Punch a hole in hinge where it covers center lacing holes (sketch c).

Punch holes in a supply of paper (choose this according to use of book) and place between covers. Lace the front

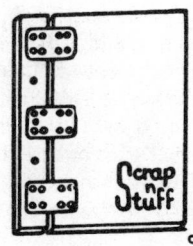

cover to the back cover with the paper between as shown in sketches d and e.

Time required to make: 2½ hours

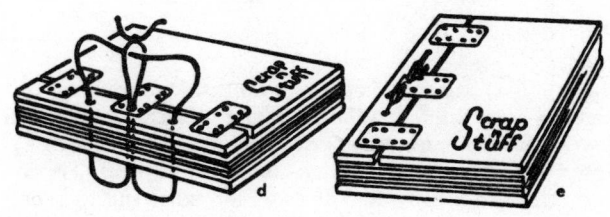

SHIP IN THE BOTTLE

Materials: Widemouth bottle with cap (catsup or milk), plaster of Paris (or putty or patching plaster), paint brush, blue poster paint, sandpaper, white thread, cloth for sail, balsa wood (or pine), sucker stick or 3/16″ dowel stick, straight pin, needle, crochet hook, glue, knife or scissors, string, thumbtack

Procedure: (1) Draw hull of boat on small piece of wood and whittle to size that will slip through neck of bottle. (2) Make a 3/16″ hole in hull of boat ½″ from front so mast will fit into it. Carve out hold (sketch a). Smooth with sandpaper. (3) Wash and dry bottle on inside. (4) Cut triangle sail 1⅝″ high by 1⅜″ wide (sketch b). (5) Cut 1¼″ mast from sucker stick or doweling. Cut one end at slight angle so mast will tip when boat is put into bottle.

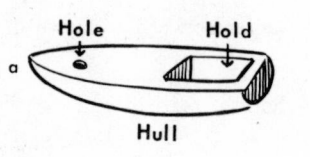

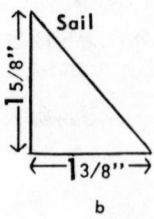

Fasten top of sail to top of mast with thread (sketch c). (6) Cut 1¼″ length of doweling for boom. Place boom at bottom of sail and attach corner at C with thread (sketch c). Insert a double thread through corner of sail at B. Tie one end of thread near bottom of mast, and other end to boom. Insert mast into hole in hull. Thumbtack a string from end of boom to back of boat. (7) Tie end of a 12″ thread to top of mast. Insert a straight pin into front end of boat

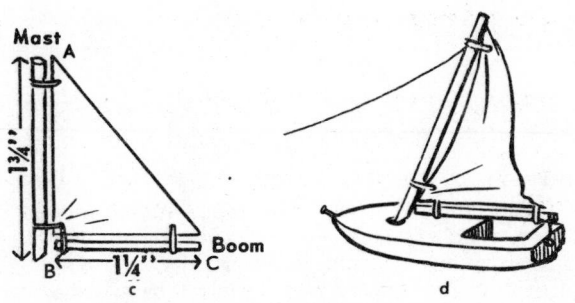

which will face bottle opening (sketch d). (8) Turn bottle on side and insert small wad of putty or plaster of Paris. Work it down along side of bottle with end of paint brush and shape to resemble waves. Paint blue. (9) Tip mast toward back of boat and collapse sail so boat will fit into bottle. Keep end of thread attached to mast *outside bottle* (sketch e). (10) Press boat firmly into position on putty or plaster, using end of paint brush or pencil. Allow to dry for 24 hours. (11) When boat is solid, gently pull thread to raise mast to upright position. With crochet hook, loop thread around pin several times. Add a drop of glue to

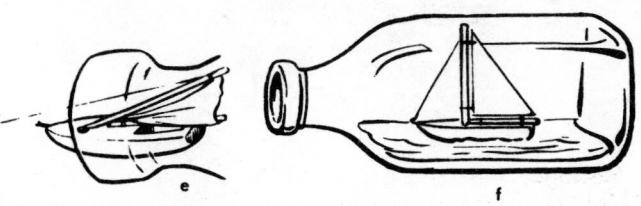

hold thread in place. When dry, cut off loose end of thread with long knife. Place cap on bottle and seal (sketch f).

Time required to make: 2 to 4 hours

SPRINKLER

Materials: Tin beverage can with bottle-cap top, or pop bottle; nail; hammer; enamel; brush; decals

Procedure: Remove cap; punch holes in top. (A clothes-sprinkler top may be obtained from a variety store and be used instead of cap.) Paint cap and can or bottle with enamel. When dry, add decals or paint on a design. Replace cap. Use for a clothes sprinkler or to douse flames in a barbecue.

Time required to make: 30 minutes plus drying time

BOY'S HAT

Materials: 1 merchandise bag 10" wide, 1 feather, glue, crayons, scissors, ruler, pencil

Procedure: Color bag. Cut off bottom 6" from closed end. Turn up 2" for band and glue. Add feather (real or paper).

Time required to make: 15 minutes

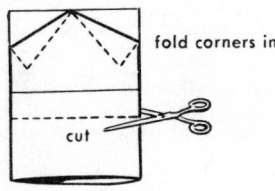

31

FOIL PICTURE

Materials: Glass cut to desired size (see directions on page 10), black enamel, colored foil or foil envelope linings, tracing paper, 1 nail or nail file, masking tape or picture frame, 1 cardboard (same size as glass), pencil, carbon paper, glue, paint brush, pictures, picture hanger

Procedure: Enamel one side of glass. Let dry. Select picture and draw or trace it on tracing paper. Place glass on table enameled side up. Lay the right side of tracing paper against enameled side of glass, so that design appears in reverse. Go over picture with firm pencil strokes so that design is marked on enamel in reverse. With nail, go over picture outline removing the enamel where foil should show through. Vary width of lines to make the picture more interesting (sketch a).

Place tracing paper right side up on cardboard. Insert carbon and transfer design to cardboard. Glue strips of colored foil on outline so colors will shine through glass where enamel has been scratched away. Place enameled side of glass next to foil. Frame picture with masking tape or a regular frame (sketch b). Add hanger on back. Create an original foil picture design such as the one in sketch c.

Time required to make: 60 minutes

a

b

c

CORK PIN AND DOG KNICKKNACK

Materials: 1 large thermos cork and 1 smaller bottle cork, 2 blue pipe cleaners, a few blue felt scraps, a few small beads, 2 thumbtacks, 1 small safety pin, scissors, white paint, 1 fine point paint brush, toothpick, Scotch tape

Procedure: Paint large cork blue for sailor body. Cut pipe cleaners in half and push ends firmly into large cork for arms and legs. Bend ends of pipe cleaners to form hands and feet. Use small cork for head. Paint white band around top of head for cap. Paint eyebrows, nose and mouth on face. For eyes, stick straight pins through small beads, then into cork. Use thumbtacks for ears. Attach head to body by inserting a toothpick halfway into cork head and then pushing rest of toothpick into body. Cut collar from felt and glue or pin to body. Scotch tape a small safety pin on back of sailor body for lapel pin.

If dog knickknack is made, use pipe cleaners for legs and tail, felt for ears, and follow same general instructions.

Time required to make: 30 to 60 minutes

BRAIDED MAT OR RUG

Materials: 3 to 6 clean nylon hose (for rug more hose or scraps of colored cloth cut into strips 1½" wide), Rit color remover and dyes, needle, thread

Procedure: Dip nylon hose in color remover, then dye desired color. Allow to dry. Cut off feet and cut tops. Cut stockings in 2" strips and sew together at ends. Sew three of these strips together to start braid. Arrange braid into circle or oval. Add strips and braid until mat is size desired. Begin at center and sew coils together. Tuck end neatly under mat and sew.

Time required to make: 30 to 50 minutes for mat, 1 to 2 hours for rug plus preparation time.

HOT PAD

Materials: Sheet cork, 9" x 4" x ½" (available at hardware, craft, hobby or art store), or nine bottle stoppers (cut in half); 28" of 18-gauge wire; wire snippers

Procedure: Cut sheet cork in pieces 1" x 2", or bottle stoppers in half lengthwise. String wire through nine pieces of cork near one end. Form into small circle, cut off excess wire and twist ends together to hold in place. Spread outer ends of cork pieces so that remaining pieces will fit between them. Lace all pieces together with wire (see sketch). Cork hot pad may be used as is or with designs painted on it.

Time required to make: 30 to 60 minutes

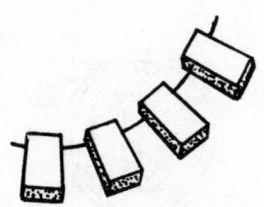

COAT RACK

Materials: 1 end of orange crate, sandpaper, 2 screw eyes, 12" heavy cord, 3 long nails with large heads, 3 large spools, hammer, enamel, brush, ruler, (optional: 3 bottle caps, 1 can top, tacks)

Procedure: Sandpaper wood. Nail 1 spool to each of three corners of the board, 1½" from edge. If nails with large heads cannot be found, flatten a bottle cap, place over spool and nail to board. Flatten nail on opposite side of the board. Attach screw eyes on the back and attach string for hanging. Enamel and paint on design. Or, stipple initials on can top and tack to rack.

Time required to make: 30 to 60 minutes

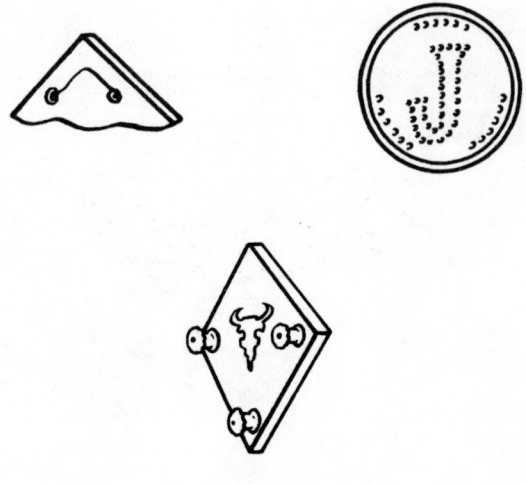

SNACK TRAY

Materials: 3 graduated sizes of spools, 3 small spools, one 8″ diameter wooden disc, one 4½″ piece of doweling, 2 nails, hammer, varnish or enamel, brush, decals, glue, pencil

Procedure: Mark center of disc on both sides. Glue doweling on one side over mark. Allow to dry. Nail doweling to disc from opposite side. Slide spools over doweling, the largest one first and smallest last. Glue securely. Varnish or enamel. Apply decals. Nail three small spools to disc for legs.

Time required to make: 60 minutes

snack tray

SHOE RACK

Materials: 1 piece of wood 10" x 10", piece of wood 8" x 16", 2 pieces of wood 1½" x 16", or 1 orange crate end and three side slats cut to the above sizes, sandpaper, 12 medium size nails, jig saw, hammer, enamel or varnish, brush, pencil, ruler, one 10" x 10" sheet of paper for pattern

Procedure: From pattern trace two sailor boys on orange crate end; cut out and sandpaper. Nail a sailor boy to each end of an 8" x 16" backboard (two side slats). Securely fasten two 1½" x 16" slats to both ends in front of rack, one right below sailor's hand and one at knee. Paint sailor boy, and varnish or enamel rest of shoe rack.

Time required to make: 1 to 1½ hours

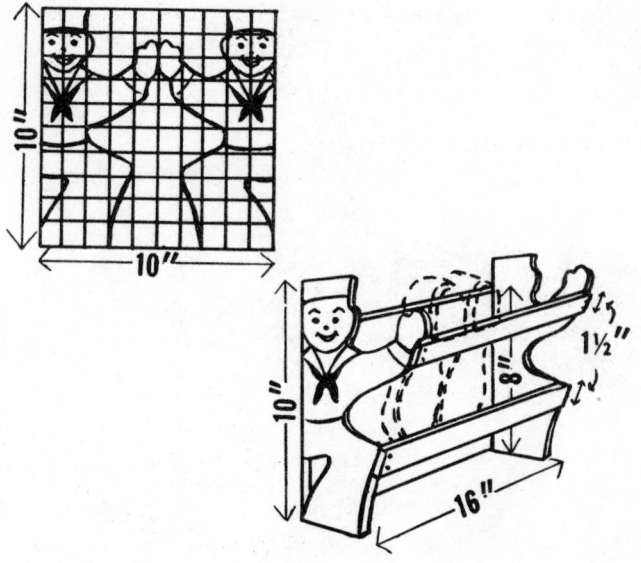

PADDLE BOAT

Materials: 1 scrap of wood 5" x 9", one 6" length of ¼" doweling, one 1½" x 2" piece of wood, jig saw, hand drill with ¼" bit, one 3½" x 6" piece of white cloth, stapler, one 7" piece of string, sandpaper, 1 heavy 4" rubber band, knife, needle and white thread, glue, sheet of 5" x 9" paper, scissors, ruler

Procedure: Trace boat pattern on wood and cut out. Sandpaper. Make a small hole 3½" from front end of boat, fill with glue and insert dowel stick for mast. Make notches on the outside of the two extending pieces at back of boat for rubber band to fit in. Cut triangular sail 3½" x 6" from cloth and attach to mast with glue or staples. Sew a string to long side of sail and staple bottom of string to boat. Use 1½" x 2" piece of wood for paddle. Stretch rubber band across back sections and insert paddle between rubber band in cutout section. Staple rubber band to middle of paddle on both sides. Twist paddle until rubber band is tight. Place boat in water and watch it go.

Time required to make: 30 minutes

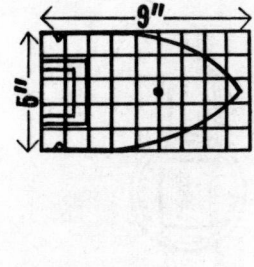

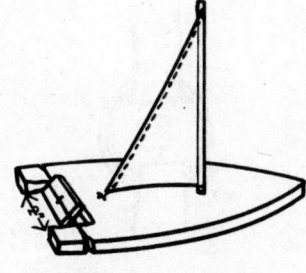

BELT MEDALLIONS

Materials: 6 can lids with ridges (removed with wall-type can opener), hammer, screw driver, knife, 20-penny nail, block of soft wood, 6 metal buttons with shank, 2 pipe cleaners, belt

Procedure: With nail and hammer punch two 1" rows of holes on opposite sides of lid. With screw driver force edges to opposite side and press down to make slits. Place on block and hammer flat. Punch two holes in center. Insert button shank from right side and run 2" piece of pipe cleaner through shank and twist end. Slide on belt.

Time required to make: 30 to 60 minutes

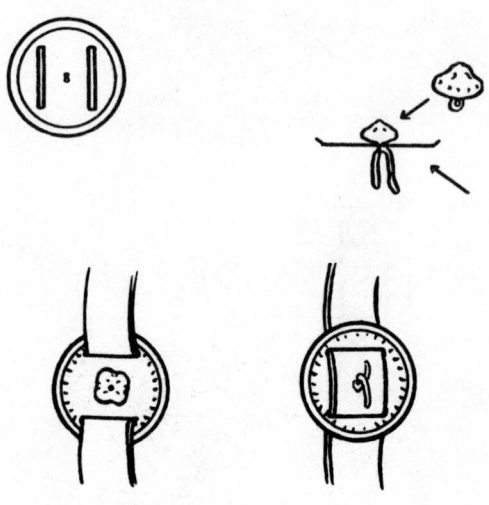

CHECKER GAME

Materials: Cardboard 12" x 12", broomstick, saw, sandpaper, red and black paint or crayons, brush

Procedure: Cut cardboard and mark off into 1½" squares (8 down and 8 across). Paint alternate squares black and allow to dry. Paint (or color) remaining squares red. Make the checkers from a broom handle by sawing 24 slices ⅜" thick. Sand checkers and paint 12 black and 12 red. (The checkers may also be cut from cardboard and colored.)

Time required to make: 30 to 60 minutes

TARGET TOSS

Materials: Large piece of wrapping paper or cardboard, yellow, red, blue and black poster paint, brush, piece of cardboard large enough to cut several arrows, scissors, sharp knife, pencil

Procedure: Make and color a large target on wrapping paper. Mark points in circles from outside to bull's-eye: 10,30,50,80,100. Cut several arrows from heavy cardboard and paint. Stand 8 feet from target, which is placed on floor and toss arrows.

Time required to make: 30 to 60 minutes

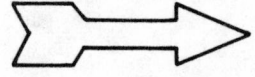

FISH BOOK END

Materials: 2 boards or wooden box ends 4" x 16", sheet of paper 8" x 10", pencil, jig saw, sandpaper, 14 medium sized nails, hammer, enamel or varnish, brush, ruler

Procedure: Saw one box end into four 4" x 4" pieces; trace fish head and tail design on two of the pieces and cut out. Sandpaper these four pieces and other box end. Nail fish head to middle of one 4" x 4" piece and tail to other piece. Securely nail fish head section to 4" x 16" base 4" from one end and tail section 4" from the opposite end. Varnish or enamel.

Time required to make: 1 to 1½ hours

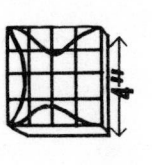 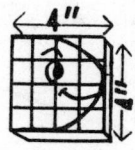

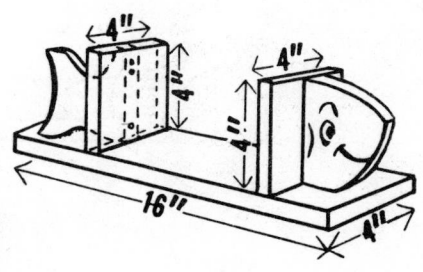

PICTURE KEYBOARD

Materials: Piece of scrap lumber 9″ x 12″, sandpaper, coping saw, 8 or 10 screw hooks, varnish or enamel, brush, magazine pictures, 2 screw eyes, glue, enough wire for hanging

Procedure: Cut wood and sandpaper. Paint or varnish it. Paste pictures on the board to identify keys. Put the screw hook near each picture. Attach the screw eyes to the back and fasten wire for hanging.

Time required to make: 30 to 60 minutes

WESTERN PURSE-N-SCARF

Materials: One and one-half 24" bandannas (cut diagonally), 24 small metal or white bone rings, needle and thread, 1 pair white 27" shoestrings, scissors

Procedure: Sew rings on wrong side of one bandanna in a circle, about 5" apart, starting approximately 1" from sides. From two opposite corners, run shoestrings through rings and tie. Hem half bandanna for scarf.

Time required to make: 30 to 60 minutes

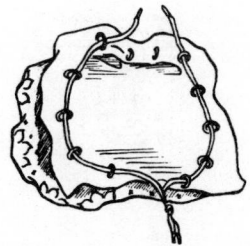

BRICK BOOK ENDS

Materials: 2 bricks, felt to cover ends of 2 bricks, scissors, pencil, ruler, rubber cement, enamel, brush, 2 decals

Procedure: Clean bricks. Enamel desired color. Let dry. Apply decals on one side of each brick or paint design. Glue felt to one end of each brick.

Time required to make: 60 minutes

TRAIL CANTEEN

Materials: Clean screw-topped bottle (syrup bottle with small handles is excellent), several thicknesses of newspaper, 1 large piece of heavy brown wrapping paper (twice the size of the bottle plus the added newspaper), scissors, 1 piece of lightweight rope long enough for large handle, pencil, Scotch tape, string, shellac

Procedure: Lay bottle on a newspaper and trace. Remove bottle and make a 1" outline around the pattern. Trace pattern on several thicknesses of newspapers and heavy wrapping paper (with one side on a fold). Cut out. Tie rope around neck of bottle (or to handles of syrup bottle) and determine length by measuring for shoulder strap. Place thicknesses of newspapers around bottle and tape. Tie papers securely. Wrap bottle in heavy wrapping paper and seal neatly with tape. Fold ends at bottom and around neck of bottle. Write name on canteen then shellac.

Time required to make: 40 minutes plus drying time

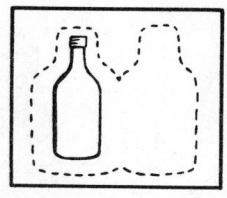

SALT AND PEPPER SHAKERS

Materials: 2 small medicine or olive bottles of the same shape with metal screw tops, two nails, one larger than the other, hammer, heavy cord, glue, shellac, scissors

Procedure: Punch three or four holes in bottle caps; use large nail for salt shaker and small one for pepper shaker. Firmly glue end of cord near bottom of bottle. Wind cord around from bottom to top over a thin layer of glue on bottle. When the top is reached, tuck end of cord under several strands and bring out and down side of bottle. Form letter "S" on one bottle and "P" on other. Glue these down firmly. Shellac bottles and allow to dry.

Time required to make: 60 minutes

BONE NECKERCHIEF SLIDE

Materials: 1" section of narrow bone, round file, flat file, sandpaper, nail file, knife, paint or indelible pencils, lacquer, brush, pan and hot water, heating unit or stove, pencil

Procedure: Boil bone and scrape clean. File outside with flat file; inside with round file. Sand with coarse sandpaper, then with fine. Sketch Indian design and carve with knife and nail file. Color design with paint or moistened indelible colored pencil. Protect design with lacquer.

Time required to make: 1 to 1½ hours

neckerchief slide

LOCKET

Materials: 1 round window shade pull with cord, enough ribbon or string to go around neck, 1 or 2 plastic or cardboard discs 1½" diameter, enough yarn or floss to wrap around ring and pull, scissors, enamel and brush, small decal or photograph, household cement.

Procedure: Bind pull with yarn or floss by wrapping yarn round and round the pull ring. Decorate disc with paint, small decal or photograph. Glue to back of bound pull so that picture is framed by the pull ring.

Variation: Use two plastic or cardboard discs. Enamel one side of each disc. Decorate enameled side of each disc with decal or design. Glue ribbon or string to back of one decorated disc. (Ribbon may be glued with ends loose to tie around neck, or ends may be glued so ribbon can be slipped over head.) Glue the discs together with glued section of ribbon between them.

Time required to make: 40 to 60 minutes

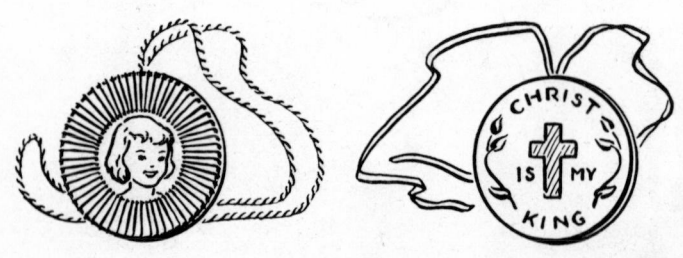

SAILOR QUOITS GAME

Materials: Heavy white cardboard 8" x 13", piece of broom handle 6" long, 32" length of ¼" rope, 1 screw eye, knife or razor blade, coping saw, piece of scrap lumber about 3" x 12", red, brown, and blue poster paint, Scotch or adhesive tape, pencil, ruler, brush, glue

Procedure: Enlarge and trace pattern for sailor head on heavy white cardboard. Paint hair brown, sailor collar blue and broom handle "nose" red. Fasten screw eye to end of 12" strip of wood and glue to back of sailor head. Nail "nose" in place from back of wood strip. Cut two 4" pieces of rope for eyes, two 2" pieces for eyebrows and one 4" length for mouth. Glue rope to face. Use remaining 16" piece of rope to make a quoit by taping ends together with adhesive or Scotch tape. (Extra quoits may be made.) Hang sailor face on wall at eye level. Object of game is to throw ring over sailor's nose.

Time required to make: 1 to 1½ hours

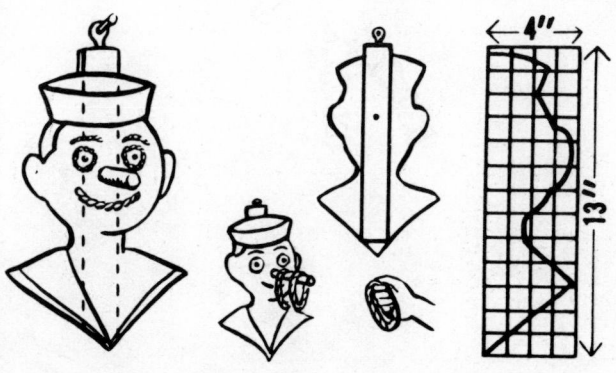

SPOOL DOLL

Materials: 12 spools (1 large one for body), soap and hot water, vegetable coloring, 3 or 4 shoestrings, large wooden beads for joints

Procedure: Wash and dip the spools in vegetable coloring and allow to dry. String spools on shoestrings. Beads may be used to help form joints. Several dolls may be made for the preschool Sunday school department.

Time required to make: 40 minutes plus drying time

PRINCESS HAT

Materials: Heavy wrapping paper 11" x 12", Scotch tape or staples, hankie or scarf

Procedure: Roll paper into cone, open end of which fits head. Fasten it with tape or staples. Attach hankie or scarf to top of hat with pin or paste.

Time required to make: 15 minutes

TREASURE CHEST

Materials: Cardboard or wooden box (with lid) about 18″ long, 9″ high, 9″ wide; 6 strips of 1½″ x 6″ heavy plastic, inner tubing or leather belts for hinges, handles and fastener; eleven 1″ paper fasteners, assorted colors of poster paints or calcimine paint, brush or wallpaper and glue, punch or nail, pencil, scissors, heavy foil

Procedure: Paint box and lid inside and out, or cover and line with wallpaper. Make a paper pattern for handles, hinges and fastener and trace on material. Cut out and make holes with punch or nail. Attach handles and fastener catch with paper fasteners. Attach fastener to lid then hinge lid to box.

Time required to make: 60 minutes

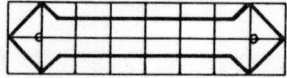

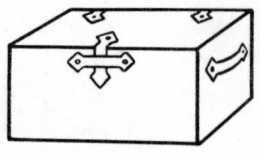

54

NAPKIN HOLDER

Materials: Cereal or other suitable box about 2"x5"x6", white cardboard (large enough for 2 boats 4" x 5"), blue, white, and brown poster paint, glue, scissors, ruler, pencil

Procedure: Cut out ends of box to within 1" of bottom and cut sides down to 3" height. Paint remaining part of box blue. Draw two boats on white cardboard and cut out. Paint hull brown. Glue boats onto sides of box about 1" from bottom of box.

Time required to make: 60 minutes

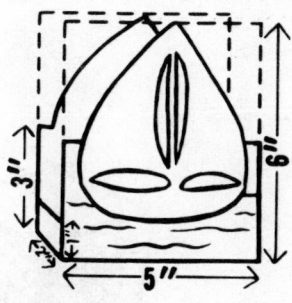

LACED WASTEPAPER BASKET

Materials: Corrugated cardboard (enough for four sides 9" x 12" x 7" and 1 bottom 7" square), paper punch, knife, pictures or paint and brush, 36" of adhesive cloth, 1 can plastic spray, 19' of plastic lacing

Procedure: Cut cardboard for bottom of wastebasket. Punch holes around edge 1" apart and ¼" in from edge. (Start ½" from corners.) Cut 4 sides like pattern. Start ½" from corners and punch holes 1" apart along 12" and 7" sides (¼" from edge). Decorate with pictures or paint. Bind 9" sides with adhesive cloth. Spray sides and bottom. Cut four 3'6" strips of lacing to lace sides together. Begin at bottom and lace like a shoe; tie at top. (See sketch.) Use bodkin to lace bottom to sides.

Time required to make: 2 hours

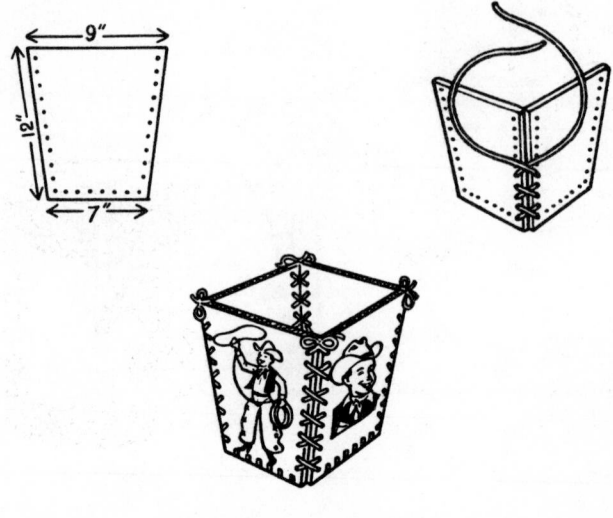

INDIAN TREASURE KEG

Materials: 1 large container with lid (such as popcorn can or five-gallon ice cream carton), 2 large sheets brown wrapping paper and paste, or buckskin colored poster paint or enamel), plastic spray (if poster paint is used), 48" medium rope, sharp object for punching holes, pencil, scissors, paint brushes

Procedure: Paper sides and lids of container with 2 layers of brown paper. Or, paint with enamel. Punch holes in side and lid for rope handle (see sketch). Trace Indian design on sides and cover; paint in bright colors. When dry spray with clear plastic spray. Insert rope handle through sides and lid; tie ends on inside of keg.

Time required to make: 60 minutes and drying time

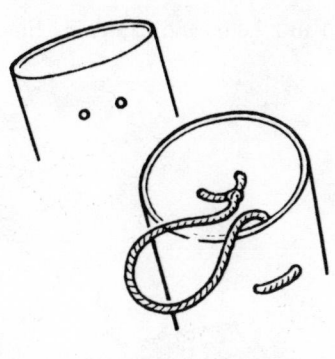

SOAP CARVING

Materials: 1 or 2 bars Ivory soap, knife, orange stick, paper napkins, toothpicks, pan of water, stove or heating unit, damp cloth

Procedure: Plan a simple design to fit bar of soap. For large figures, join 2 bars. To do this, slice thin layer from sides to be joined; place bars, cut sides down, in shallow pan of water over low heat. Allow soap to soften 15 minutes; remove, insert toothpicks where they will not interfere with carving and press soft sides of bars together. Allow 24 hours for hardening.

Before carving, scrape soap to make smooth surface. Trace design on bar with orange stick. Cut away soap to within ¼″ of design. Carve details. Smooth rough places with a damp cloth; let dry 24 hours. To polish, rub with a paper napkin, then with palm of hand.

Time required to make: 1 to 2 hours and hardening time

CANDLE MOLDING

Materials: Scraps of old candles, Jello molds and/or frozen fruit juice or baby food cans, string, old sauce pan, electric hot plate, vegetable coloring, doilies, greeting cards, glitter, sequins, scissors, 1 pencil for each mold, warm water

Procedure: Melt candles in saucepan. Cut wicks from string, 2" longer than needed. Color wax with vegetable coloring. Pour into Jello molds. Tie wicks to pencils and place over molds so wicks are in center. (Several pieces of string may be used for stamens.) Let wax harden. Remove candle. (Dip mold in warm water first.) Candles will float.

To decorate the Jello mold candles, press sequins or glitter into the warm wax while still in the mold. To decorate the can-shaped candles, cut designs from the greeting cards and press into the side of the candle, then set it on a doily.

Time required to make: 30 to 60 minutes

LOOM MAT

Materials: One 6" square cardboard, pencil, scissors, Scotch tape, rug yarn, needle, string, ruler

Procedure: Draw a line ¼" inside cardboard square. Mark off every ½" along inside frame and cut a V to each point. Tape end of yarn to back of cardboard and start at lower left corner to wind yarn up and down around notches. Turn loom and wind yarn crosswise. Continue weaving until there is a 4-strand thickness. Thread needle with string and make buttonhole stitch up and down the rows. Secure thread. Clip mat from loom (from back) and trim starting yarn.

Time required to make: 30 minutes

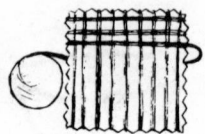
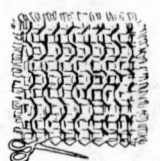

FOIL PLAQUE

Materials: 1 foil plate 8" or 9" diameter, sharpened stick, 10" yarn or ribbon, poster paints, paint brush, pencil, 1 sheet typing paper, newspaper, Scotch tape, carbon paper, table knife, scissors

Procedure: Cut paper to fit inside of foil plate. Print words, "Follow Me," on paper and any desired decoration. Trace design on opposite side of paper by holding paper to window, or by using carbon paper with carbon side to back of design. Smooth out any design in foil plate with knife handle. Stuff plate with newspapers. Tape design to back of plate, right side down and trace with sharp stick. Paint plate. Punch holes in top rim and attach bow for hanging.

Time required to make: 60 minutes

INDIAN DOLL

Materials: Child's red sock size 7, needle, red thread, black embroidery thread, scissors, cotton, 1 strip of colored cloth 7½" x 1½", piece of ribbon to fit around head, rubber band, 1 small feather, crayons, ruler

Procedure: Cut sock 2½" from toe. Cut toe section in half to make arms. Fold sock foot flat and cut to within 2" of heel to make legs. Turn wrong side out and sew around legs. Turn arm pieces and sew, leaving wide ends open. Turn body and arms and stuff with cotton. Gather top of sock and sew. Tie several strands of black thread around legs and arms ½" from ends (for feet and hands), and 2½" from top of sock for head. Sew on arms. Draw face with black crayon. Loop embroidery thread, cut and tie, then sew to top of head. Tack ribbon around head and insert feather. Fringe and color a strip of colored cloth and slip under rubber band at waist for loincloth.

Variation: Dolls representing children from all the world can be made by using different colored socks and changing the dress a little.

Time required to make: 1 to 1½ hours

BROOCH

Materials: Heavy cardboard or plastic disc 1½" in diameter, enamel, 1 small decal, paint brush, 1 small safety pin, 1 yard heavy thread, 1 small block of wood 1" x ½" x 3/16", household cement, 1 round shade pull, yarn, beads, lace, etc. (use in addition to above materials in variation)

Procedure: If cardboard is to be used, cut circle. Coat heavily with enamel and let dry. Apply small decal in center of cardboard or plastic disc, or paint original design (sketch a).

Open safety pin and bind with thread to small block of wood (sketch b). Glue block of wood with pin attached to back of disc (sketch c). Allow to dry thoroughly before wearing.

Variation: Decorate a round shade pull as a frame for the brooch, using yarn, small beads, lace, etc. Glue decorated shade pull to disc so picture is framed by shade pull.

Time required to make: 30 to 60 minutes

FOOTLOCKER

Materials: Wooden or cardboard box with lid
9"x 13"x 9", 2 strips 2" x 4" and 4 strips of heavy plastic
1½" x 2", inner tubing or leather belts; 2 pieces of rope
8" long, tacks or paper fasteners, ice pick, paint or enamel,
varnish, brush, hammer, ruler, pencil

Procedure: Paint box and lid inside and out. Hinge lid
to box with two 2" x 4" strips. Use paper fasteners for
cardboard boxes and tacks for wooden boxes. Tie knots in
ends of two rope pieces. Attach one end of two 1½" x 2"
strips to sides of box about 4" apart. Place rope handles
under strips and attach other ends of strips to box tightly
enough so knots will not slip through (see sketch). Paint
name or initials on box. A foil motto or crest may be attached to lid or side of box.

Time required to make: 1 to 2 hours plus drying time

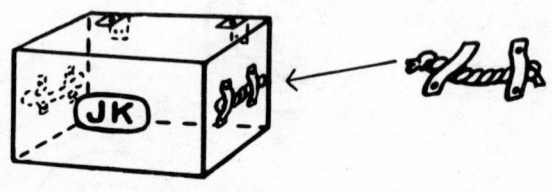

INDIAN CATCH GAME

Materials: Piece of paper 6" x 11", pencil, piece of heavy cardboard or ⅜" plywood 6" x 11", knife, razor blade or coping saw, sandpaper, poster paints or enamel, brush, piece of string 18" long

Procedure: Enlarge pattern from sketch. Trace on heavy cardboard and cut out. Or, trace on ⅜" plywood and cut out with coping saw. Sandpaper. Paint face on both sides. Cut cardboard circle. Tie one end of string to circle and other end to Indian. Hold Indian by neck, toss circle into air and try to catch it on feather.

Time required to make: 30 to 50 minutes plus drying time

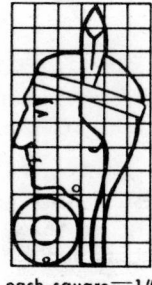

each square = 1"

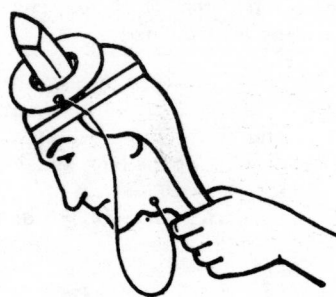

BREADBOARD, CHOPPING BOARD

Materials: 1 orange crate end, sandpaper, coping saw

Procedure: Trace outline on wood and cut out with coping saw. Sandpaper until smooth.

Time required to make: 30 to 60 minutes

SPICE SACHET

Materials: Two 4" squares of small mesh netting, 1 yard colored yarn or ribbon, enough cloves and pieces of dried apple to fill netting

Procedure: Cut netting any shape desired. Lace netting together along 3 sides with yarn or ribbon. Mix dried apples and cloves and place between netting and complete lacing. Tie lacing in bow and loop over hanger.

Time required to make: 30 minutes

BIBLE COVER

Materials: Enough felt, plastic or leather to generously cover closed Bible, plus a 5″ strip the height of the Bible, scissors, pencil, ruler, punch, narrow ribbon or plastic lacing, scraps of contrasting material or leather, tooling instrument, glue, needle and thread, heavy weight, paper clips

Procedure: Measure your Bible, then cut a cover that will fit all around closed Bible and extend ½″ on each side. Cut two flaps of the same material about 2½″ wide and the same height as the Bible. Plan design for front cover. (Do leather tooling before putting cover together.) Lay cover flat, wrong side up and clip flaps at each end of cover with paper clips (see sketch). Punch holes all around cover ½″ apart and ¼″ from edge. Make the first two holes at each corner only ¼″ apart (see sketch). Start lacing at center bottom and lace all around cover, lacing flaps in place to form pockets. Use either an overcast or blanket stitch. Use ribbon for felt covers and plastic lacing for plastic or leather covers. Overlap ends of lacing and tie or sew in place. Slip book into cover. Cut out design in contrasting colors for felt or plastic covers and sew or glue in place. If design is glued to cover, allow it to dry over night under a weight.

Time required to make: 1 to 2 hours plus drying time

BOOK OF BIBLE ARROWS

Materials: 1 piece 12" x 18" colored construction paper, ruler, scissors, 10" colored yarn, pencil

Procedure: Fold paper lengthwise in five equal folds, accordion fashion. Crease, then fold in half. Draw arrow on folded paper making sure that end is on fold. Cut out. Pupils may trade arrows to have different colors. Overlap arrows and tie with yarn. Print on the cover: "BIBLE ARROWS that Will Kill the Enemies in My Life." On each page write, "To kill (name an enemy)." Below the name write a suitable verse.

Time required to make: 30 minutes

SWORD OF TRUTH

Materials: Piece of cardboard 5" x 20", 1" paper fastener, foil, glitter, colored buttons, several strips of colored construction paper 1¼" x 14", thumbtacks, glue or needle and thread, scissors, jig saw

Procedure: Enlarge pattern of sword to dimensions given. Trace on cardboard and cut out. Cover with foil or paint. Decorate hilt by studding with "jewels" of colored buttons, glitter, etc. (sewed or glued on). Provide pupil with 1¼" x 14" strip of colored construction paper. Taper one end to represent blade point. When pupil learns verses he may write them, from memory, on the blades and fasten to back of sword with paper fastener. Use different colored paper. The fastener becomes the center jewel in the cross bar of the sword. If schools have jig saws, pupil may cut swords from orange crates (or plywood) and gild them. Put colored thumbtacks in hilt for jewels.

Time required to make: 60 minutes

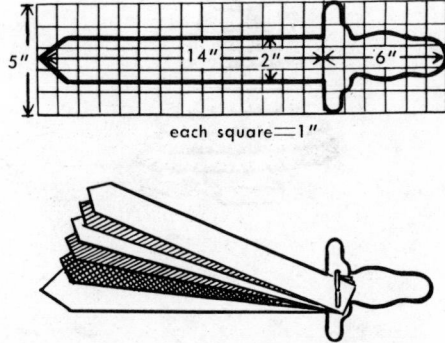

each square = 1"

CHRISTMAS TREE

Materials: Several pieces of colored construction paper, compass, scissors, ⅛" doweling, block of wood for stand, Scotch tape, pencil, 1 star for top of tree

Procedure: Cut about 14 circles of graduating size from construction paper. Snip around outside edge of circles. Push dowel through center of graduated circles with smallest one at the top. Space circles evenly along dowel and fasten with Scotch tape. Make hole in block and stand tree upright. Star may be added at the top.

Time required to make: 30 to 60 minutes

CHRISTMAS DECORATIONS

Materials: Hammer, several tin cans, tin snips, pencil, punch, cord, file, glue, glitter

Procedure: Flatten out tin cans and cut into strips ¼" wide. Wrap around pencil in spiral and remove. Punch hole in end. Attach cord and hang on tree.

Cut ends from cans. Smooth edges of discs with file and punch hole near rim. Dip in glue and then in glitter. Attach to cord and use on tree.

Time required to make: 30 to 60 minutes

HANGING PLANTER

Materials: 3 aluminum foil pie tins (3" diameter), four 18" lengths No. 3 round "strapping" copper or aluminum wire, 1 small nail, 1 cup hook, 1 small block of wood 1" x 1" x ⅜" or ½", stapler, 1 plant, enough soil to fill 1 pan

Procedure: With nail, punch eight evenly spaced holes around the bottom of two tins (sketch a). Place small block of wood in center of one perforated tin. Screw cup hook through outside of pie tin into block of wood so they fit together tightly. Bend wires in U shape to fit the space between the holes (sketch b). Insert bent wires through top of tin with cup hook attached. After all wires are in place, bend each wire in 2" from bottom (sketch c). Put these wires through corresponding holes in other perforated pie tin. Work carefully so aluminum foil will not tear. After wires are all in place, fit unperforated pan under the bottom tin to cover wire ends and make a solid bottom. Staple the two bottom tins together around the edge of rims. Now shape the wires to give a Japanese lantern effect (sketch d). Fill bottom pan with soil, and plant vine or plant in soil.

Time required to make: 30 to 40 minutes

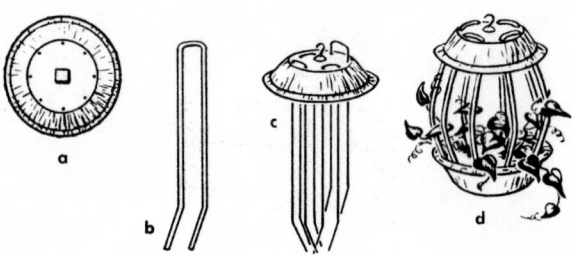

72

LOG CABIN SETTLEMENT

Materials: 1 roll of corrugated paper, paper clips, paper fasteners, toothpicks, scissors, knife, glue, cardboard boxes, clay, pieces of shrubs

Procedure: Let pupils use their ingenuity to create a pioneer settlement. Make log cabins from corrugated paper used horizontally. Cut corrugated paper vertically for stockades. Place toothpicks in some of corrugations for pickets. Cut lookout windows with knife. Small boxes may be covered with glue and then with toothpicks for log buildings. Put bits of shrubs in clay for trees.

Time required to make: 1 to 3 hours

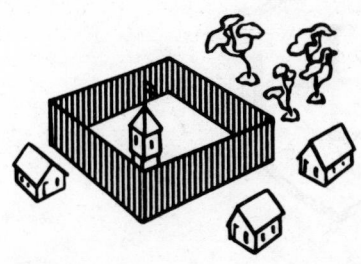

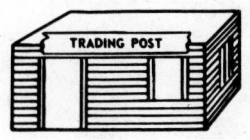

73

SHIELD

Materials: Piece of cardboard 18″ x 24″, 2 strips of cloth 2″ x 7″, paints, glue or stapler, scissors, ruler, pencil

Procedure: Draw a shield on cardboard and cut out. Draw on design and paint. Staple or glue strips of cloth across the back in upper right corner and in center. Forearm slips through lower loop and hand grips upper one.

Time required to make: 30 to 60 minutes

back

SEMAPHORE FLAGS

Materials: Two 12" squares of muslin or sheeting, 1 red wax crayon, 2 dowel sticks 16" long, thumbtacks, white thread, needle, pencil, scissors, newspaper, hot iron.

Procedure: Sew a ¼" hem on all sides of cloth. Draw a diagonal line between two corners on each flag and color one-half of it with red wax crayola. Place colored side down on newspaper and "set color" with a hot iron. Tack to dowel stick.

Time required to make: 30 to 60 minutes

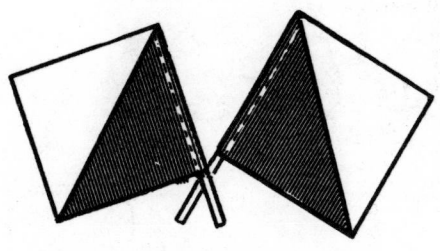

RICKRACK JEWELRY

Materials: Two 11½" lengths of rickrack in harmonizing or contrasting colors for each earring or pin, needle, thread, ¾" earring base or safety pin, small pearl or rhinestone button, glue, scissors

Procedure: Sew ends of each piece of rickrack together. Overlap rickrack and sew together, catching each pair of points. Pull thread tightly and sew rosette. Glue a pearl or rhinestone in center. Sew pin to back or glue to earring base.

Time required to make: 30 to 60 minutes

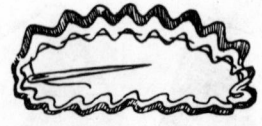

CANISTER SET

Materials: 3 coffee tins with lids, ½, 1 and 2-pound sizes, enamel, brush, pictures in color from magazines, etc., clear nail polish or shellac, scissors

Procedure: Paint outside of tins and lids with enamel. While paint is wet, press on pictures. After enamel is dry, coat pictures with clear nail polish or shellac.

Time required to make: 30 to 60 minutes plus drying time

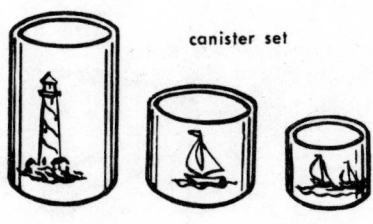

canister set

FOOTSTOOL

Materials: 1 shallow wooden box 10" x 15", four 9"
lengths of doweling, 20 large-sized spools, 4 bottle caps,
glue, 12 finishing nails, 4 small nails with large heads,
scissors, ¾ yard cretonne, drapery material, or plastic;
padding, upholstery tacks, hammer, one 3" x 3" felt scrap

Procedure: Box should have bottom and four sides. Glue
one spool inside each corner. Dip end of each dowel in glue
and place in a spool. When dry, slip four more spools
over each dowel. Make a hole in center of bottle caps and
nail one to each leg. Turn stool over and nail legs securely,
making sure that one nail is hammered into doweling. Pad
top of stool and tack covering on under side of stool,
stretching it firmly. Varnish legs. Cut and glue felt on bottom of legs.

Time required to make: 30 to 60 minutes

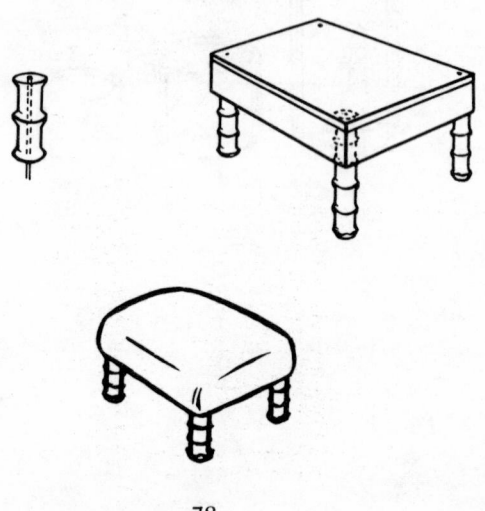

PICTURE BOARD OR TACK BOARD

Materials: Piece of double corrugated box 18" x 24" (or desired size), 30 to 40 spools (same size), poster paint, brush, sharp knife, small hammer, glue, enamel, brush, 2 cloth suspension rings, ruler, pencil

Procedure: Cut spools in half by placing sharp knife on end of each spool and hitting with hammer. Cut 4 halves diagonally to use at corners. Enamel spools. Trim cardboard and paint. Glue dry spools along edges of board. Attach suspension rings for hanging.

Time required to make: 2 to 3 hours

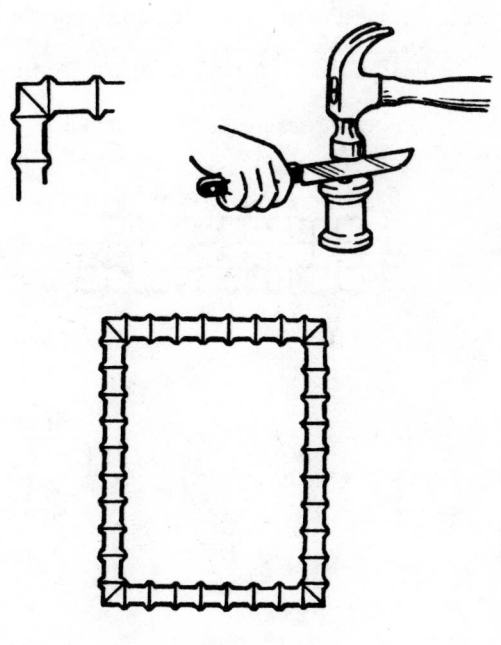

SUNBONNET SEWING KIT

Materials: Piece of cardboard 2½" x 6", piece of 6" x 12" printed percale, piece plain color flannel 4" x 5", needle, thread, scissors, pinking shears, pencil

Procedure: Enlarge pattern and cut 2 bonnet brims from cardboard and flannel and 2 double brims of percale. Trim cardboard ⅛" on all sides and place inside cloth brim pieces. Sew cloth edges together. Cut 2 sides of flannel with pinking shears and sew plain side to corresponding side of brim.

Cut 6" square of percale for crown. Trim corners round and hem. Gather one side ½" from edge and draw thread so width of cloth measures 1". Start 2" from gathered end and make running stitch, ½" from edge, around rest of crown to within 2" from gathered end. Draw thread until gathered area is 2". Sew crown to brims. Thimble and thread will fit in crown; flannel is for pins and needles.

Time required to make: 30 to 60 minutes

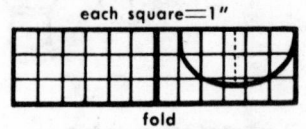

each square=1"

fold

PAPOOSE PIN

Materials: Finger of old leather glove, piece of cardboard 2" x 5", enough patching plaster to make a ¾" diameter ball, glue, enough cotton to fill finger of glove, black and white embroidery thread, 1 safety pin, red watercolor pencil, black paint, scissors, Scotch tape, ruler

Procedure: Make a ¾" diameter ball of patching plaster for head of papoose and insert piece of cardboard ½" x 2". Cut finger from glove and rip one side to 2" from end, then cut across 1¼". Round one end of a piece of cardboard ¾" x 2¼" and insert into finger. Fold end and side of glove over cardboard and glue. Color papoose head red. Paint face. Loop and tie several strands of black embroidery thread then paste to head for hair. Wrap cotton around cardboard to fill finger. Slip papoose in holder and tie with white thread. Tape safety pin to back.

Time required to make: 30 minutes

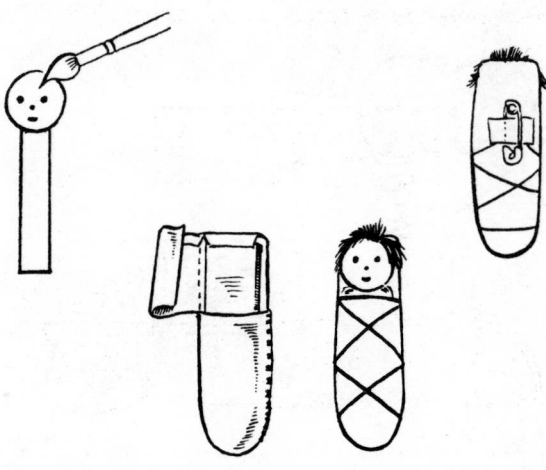

PERSONALIZED PINS

Materials: Soft copper wire (about 12″ for a four-letter name), pointed pliers, scissors or pinking shears, needle, thread, colored felt scraps, cork or wood, 1 small safety pin, pencil

Procedure: Bend wire to form name (use pliers for sharp bends). Cut felt into any desired shape large enough to be used as a background for the name. (Edges may be pinked for a more decorative effect.) Sew the name on the felt background and attach small safety pin to back. Pupil may make extra pins for gifts.

(Note: Boys may wish to mount their names on cork or wood and attach them to their personal belongings.) These wire names also may be used for original and unusual place cards for a dinner or party.

Time required to make: 30 to 60 minutes

KNITTING BAG

Materials: Rolled oats box, wallpaper or pictures, glue, enamel, brush, 15" piece of lightweight rope, 3 gummed reinforcements, scissors

Procedure: Cover rolled oats box and lid with wallpaper or paint. If painted, press individual pictures onto wet paint. Cut one small round hole in center of lid and on opposite sides of box about 2" from top. Paste gummed reinforcements over holes on inside of box to strengthen them. Make rope handle by putting rope through holes and tying knots inside of box. Yarn is placed inside box and one end drawn through hole in lid before knitting is begun. Or, foil designs may be glued to painted box.

Time required to make: 30 to 60 minutes

SCARF AND TIE RACK

Materials: Piece of white cardboard 8" square, metal coat hanger, heavy cord, glue, shellac, brush, scissors, Scotch tape, pencil

Procedure: Wrap cord around wire all along hanger triangle over a thin coat of glue. Shellac and allow to dry. Draw an 8" diameter life preserver on cardboard with a 3" hole. Then cut out. Cut through one side of life preserver so it can be slipped on hanger. Scotch tape life preserver together and fasten to hanger (underneath hook) by wrapping cord around side of life preserver and tying to hook (see sketch). Tie three other cords around life preserver as shown in sketch.

Time required to make: 30 to 60 minutes

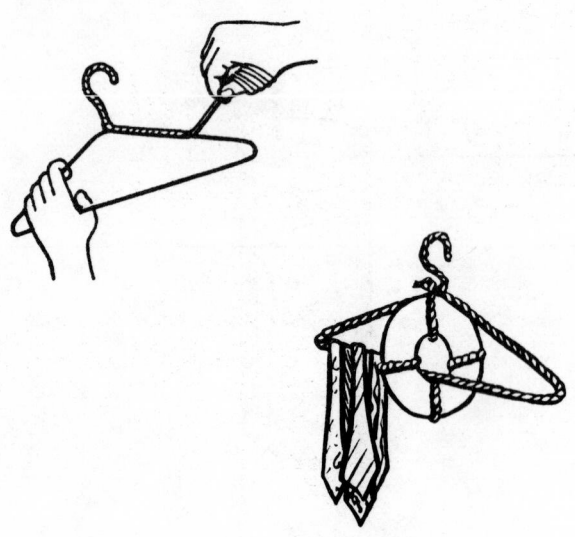

SHIELD OF FAITH PLAQUE

Materials: Piece of colored construction paper 6" x 7", pencil, ruler, piece of heavy paper 3" x 5", glue, glitter, piece of colored cardboard 9" x 12", cloth suspension hanger

Procedure: Trace cross on heavy paper and cut out. Cover cross with glue; sprinkle with glitter. Enlarge shield pattern and trace on construction paper. Paste cross on shield. Mount shield on cardboard. Print "Shield of Faith" at top of plaque and Ephesians 6:16 at bottom. Attach hanger to back.

Time required to make: 30 minutes

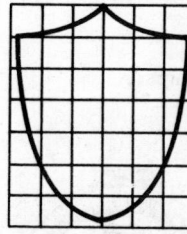 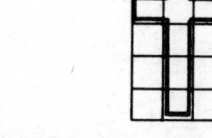

each square = 1"

WALL VASE

Materials: 1 paper or aluminum foil plate, 1 plastic or glass toothbrush tube, 24" narrow ribbon, decals, stickers or pictures, paper punch or sharp stick, household cement, 2 sheets colored construction paper (different colors), 1 sheet typing paper, scissors, pen or pencil

Procedure: Decorate plate in any manner desired. Place tube in center of plate and mark places for holes on either side of tube near top and bottom (see sketch). Punch holes. Glue tube between holes in plate.

Print Bible verse on piece of white paper. Make a double mounting of colored construction paper and glue verse in center. Run 7" strip of ribbon around tube and through holes in bottom of plate and glue ends behind memory verse so it will hang below plate. Run rest of ribbon around tube and through holes at top to make hanger for wall vase. Tie ends in bow.

Time required to make: 30 to 40 minutes

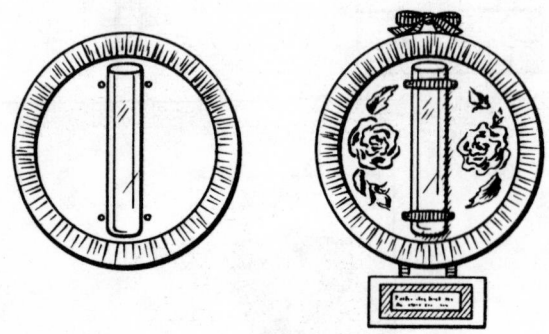

PAPIER-MACHE PLAQUES

Materials: Papier-mache (recipe on page 115); piece of wood 5½" x 6½"; wood stain; 2 brushes; 2½" length adhesive tape; 4" length of string; glue; poster paints or vegetable food coloring

Procedure: Stain wood base and allow to dry. Decide what kind of design is to be made on plaque. Sketch design on wood and cover this area with glue before molding papier-mache in place (sketch a). When molding is finished, allow 2 or 3 days for papier-mache to dry (sketch b). Then paint the molded object as desired with poster paints or food coloring (sketch c). When paint is dry, attach hanger. Knot each end of the string and place in loop fashion on back of plaque, near top. Tape loop to board (see sketch d).

Time required to make: 1 to 2 hours plus drying time

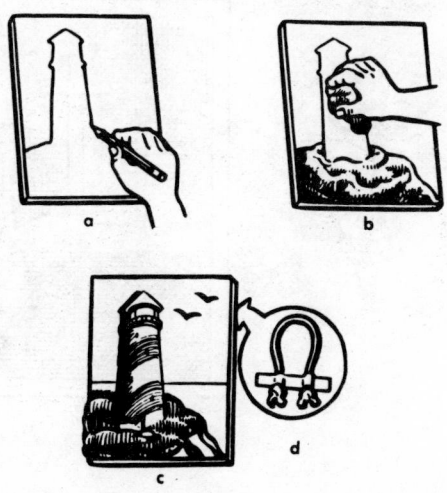

WIRE SCREEN PICTURES

Materials: 1 piece of wire screen approximately 7"x10" (or according to available screen from stores or friends), enough colored adhesive tape to bind edges, assorted colors of yarn, blunt darning needle

Procedure: Bind edges of screen with tape. Thread the darning needle with colored yarn and stitch a design on the screen. The design may be related to V.B.S. lessons or theme, illustrate a Bible verse, etc. Several colors of yarn make the picture effective. Encourage originality.

Time required to make: 1 to 2 hours

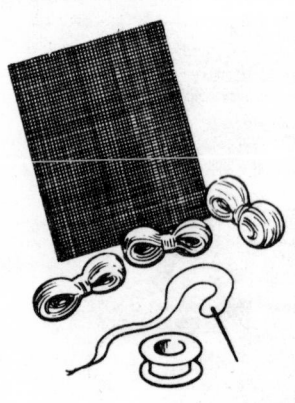

FISH MOBILES

Materials: Wire snippers, metal coat hanger (light-weight), tape, copper pot cleaner, paper fasteners, gummed reinforcements, mesh raveling

Procedure: Snip hook from hanger, leaving one long strip of wire when straightened. Make sharp bend near center, then two reverse bends 1" from first to form mouth of fish. Cross wire about 4" from ends to form tail. Make bends in tail so ends of wire meet. Tape ends together. Two small fish may be made from one hanger. Suspend fish from ceiling by thread.

Variation: Cover fish with copper pot cleaner to make glistening scales. Remove fastener from cleaner and stretch it over the fish. Tie it around fish's tail with a mesh raveling. Put paper fasteners through gummed reinforcements for eyes.

Time required to make: 30 to 60 minutes

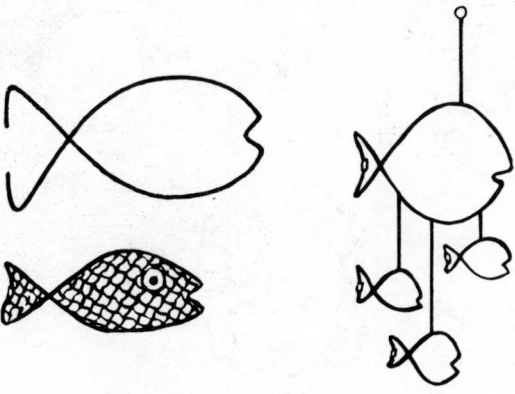

HEADBAND

Materials: 4 or 5 pipe cleaners, piece of material 5¾" x 26" (starched curtain net, taffeta, etc.), bobby pins, artificial flowers, needle and thread, scissors, ruler

Procedure: Twist pipe cleaners together end to end to fit around head, halo style. Gather material 3¼" from one side to make ruffle in two tiered layers. Arrange ruffle around two-thirds of halo and tack in place. Flowers may be added at either end of ruffles. Use bobby pins to hold in place.

Time required to make: 30 minutes

TROPHY BOARD

Materials: 2 long sides of orange crate, saw, piece of heavy cardboard or tackboard the length of the crate, small nails or long carpet tacks, sandpaper, varnish, tan and brown paint, woodburning set, brush, 2 screw eyes, enough wire to hang board, pencil

Procedure: Cut sides of crate in four 3" strips to fit around cardboard. Cut ends of all pieces at 45° angle for corners. Sandpaper. Draw a stretched hide on cardboard. Paint hide tan and rest of cardboard brown. Burn a western design and name in wood. Tack to edges of cardboard. Put screw eyes in back. Attach wire for hanging.

Time required to make: 60 minutes

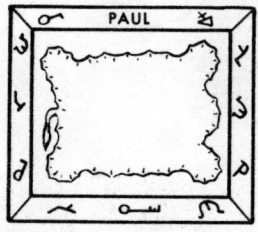

BRACELET

Materials: Tongue depressor, ready-mixed moist gesso,*
enamel, brushes, can 2½" in diameter with both ends removed

Procedure: Soak tongue depressor in water overnight.
Coat depressor with gesso. Bend carefully and fit inside can.
Let dry about 24 hours. Remove bracelet from can; enamel
any color. Add design in contrasting color.

Time required to make: 30 to 50 minutes plus drying
time

* Available from a hobby store.

WHITTLE PLAQUE

Materials: Sharp knife, 5 sticks 8″ x 1½″ (or twigs equivalent size), woodburning set, 30″ long heavy cord, varnish, brush, scissors

Procedure: Whittle sticks smooth and make notch 1″ from ends. Choose a motto and woodburn words on sticks. Varnish. Link plaque together by tying cord around notches.

Time required to make: 30 to 60 minutes

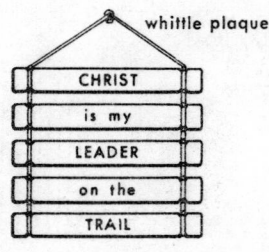
whittle plaque

WAGON WHEEL HOT PAD

Materials: 29 ice cream sticks or wooden coffee stirrers, 3/32" twist drill, ruler, pencil, 29 wooden beads or round corks ⅜" diameter, long-nosed pliers, shellac, brush, 24" wire

Procedure: In each stick drill a hole 3/16" from end and another hole 2" from the first. (See sketch.) Be sure holes in each stick are exactly the same distance apart. Run wire through the end hole of all 29 sticks keeping them upright. Pull wire tight and fasten securely with long-nosed pliers. String beads between remaining holes. (See sketch.) Fasten wire and clip ends. Hot pads may be shellacked.

Time required to make: 1 to 1½ hours

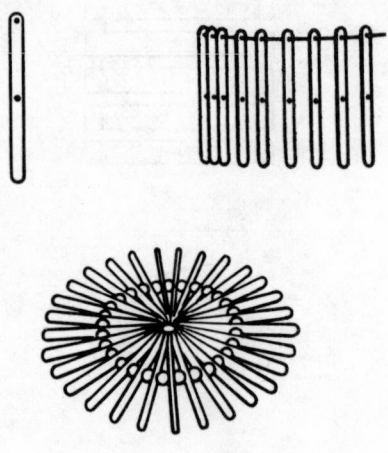

HOUSE NUMBER SIGN

Materials: End of 1 orange crate, scrap of wood 2" x 12", sandpaper, coping saw, enamel, brush, house numbers, finishing nails, pencil, ruler

Procedure: Draw design on wood. Cut out with coping saw. Cut stake piece 12" x 2" with pointed end. Sandpaper and paint. Tack numbers on "house" or numbers may be painted. Nail stake to back of sign.

Time required to make: 30 to 60 minutes

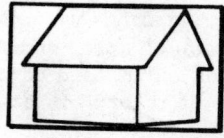

JET SCOOTER

Materials: 1 roller skate, 4 pieces of lumber in the following sizes, 12" x 27", 3½" x 27", 3½" x 10", 2" x 17"; 10 to 15 large nails, hammer, saw, sandpaper, paint, brush, ruler

Procedure: Separate the two sections of skate. Nail back part of skate to one end of the 3½" x 27" piece of lumber. (Hammer nails in part way and bend over skate to hold it firmly.) Nail 3½" x 10" piece of lumber about 3½" from other end of this piece. Nail front section of skate at end of shorter piece of lumber.

Place the section with skate attached in center of 12" x 27" piece of lumber. Insert the 2" x 17" piece crosswise between the two other sections about 4" from front end. This makes a sled-type steering bar. (See sketch.) Hammer spike nails through platform of scooter and steering bar into skate section, fastening firmly. Sand edges of platform and steering bar. Paint or decorate if desired. Ride scooter in kneeling position.

Time required to make: 2 hours

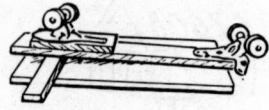

FOIL FRAME

Materials: 1 aluminum foil pie tin, scissors, pencil
For alternate style: 2 aluminum foil pie tins the same size, scissors, stapler, pencil

Procedure: Score the bottom of 1 pie tin into 8 equal pieces (see sketch a). Cut the lines across the bottom of the tin but do not cut the sides. Starting at the center, roll each "slice" around a pencil back to the sides (sketch b). This gives the rounded effect. Place tin with the widest side down on picture. Glue or staple the picture to edge of foil tin. For style 2: Fix 1 pie tin as directed above. Then staple it to another uncut tin brim to brim (sketch c). Place 3-D flowers, pictures or other articles in it (sketch d).

Time required to make: 10 to 20 minutes

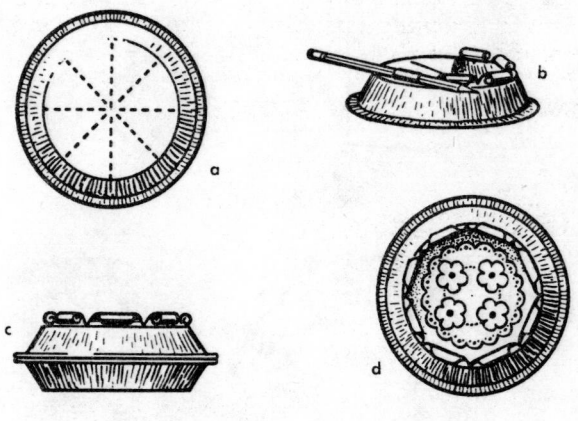

97

MESH HELMET

Materials: Paper bag to fit head, 1 large copper pot cleaner, stapler, needle

Procedure: Cut paper bag off 3" from bottom. Turn under 1" hem on bottom piece to form base of helmet. Unstaple pot cleaner and carefully stretch to full size. Cut out a 7" square of mesh to make an opening for the face about 2" from one end of mesh tube. With a strand of pot cleaner, weave this square into top of pot cleaner tube. Now slip paper-bag helmet base into closed end of mesh tube and staple in place. Slip helmet on head with face in opening and let mesh hang loosely around head.

Time required to make: 1 hour

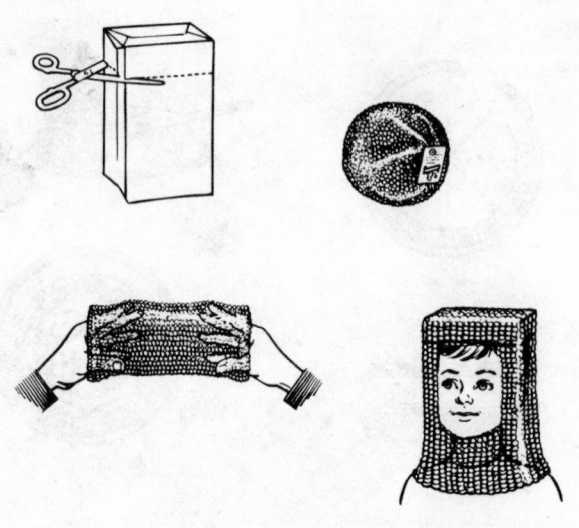

CRUSADER TUNIC

Materials: Pillowcase or white feed sack, 2 copper pot cleaners, red crayon, pencil, needle and thread

Procedure: Rip open seam in end of pillowcase to make opening large enough so head will slip through. Rip open seams down the sides for 7" to make armholes. Secure threads at ends of openings. Sketch a cross on front of tunic in pencil and color with crayons. Press on wrong side over damp cloth with hot iron to set color. Carefully unstaple pot cleaner and unroll. Stretch to full size. Sew to armhole. Make 2nd sleeve in same manner. Tunic may be worn loose or belted. Wear mesh helmet and carry sword.

Time required to make: 1 hour

T SHIRT

Sketch cross or coat of arms on front of shirt in pencil. Color with crayons. Press on wrong side over damp cloth with iron to set colors. Let dry.

Time required to make: 1 hour

SWORD

Cut from ⅜" wood (approximately 4"x18"), using original pattern. Sand, varnish and decorate as desired.

Time required to make: 1 to 2 hours

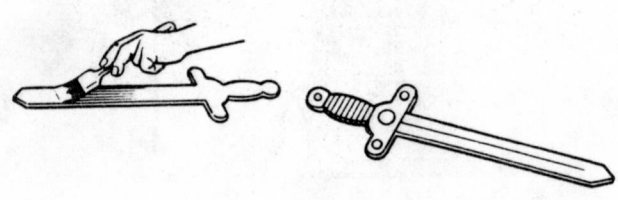

RELIEF MAP

Materials: Soapsuds paint (see page 113), waxed paper, piece of plywood or heavy cardboard size of map desired, sandpaper or binding tape, knife, flat sucker stick, paint, paintbrush, pencil

Procedure: Bind the edge of cardboard for map base, or sand edges of plywood. Outline map on board with pencil. Apply soapsuds paint in layers to show topography of country, such as Palestine, Bible Lands, Mediterranean Lands, etc. Slightly moisten hands when shaping mountains, etc.

Fresh soapsuds paint can be added to the dry part without danger of cracking. Be sure to allow each layer to dry before applying the next. Use the knife and stick to draw in rivers, shape mountains, etc. When dry, paint lakes, rivers, mountains, etc.

Time required to make: About 2 hours

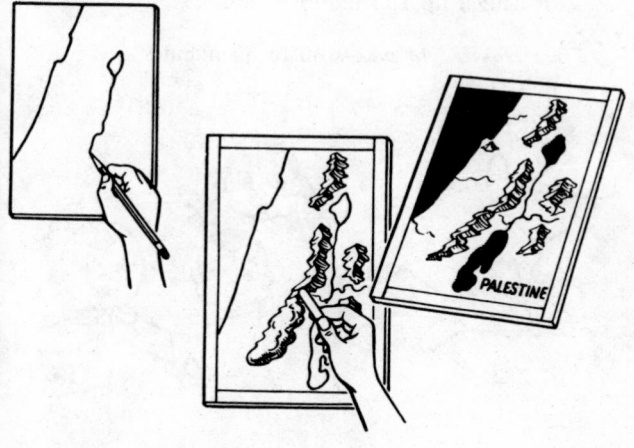

PERSONALITY TIE OR RIBBON RACK

Materials: 1 wire coat hanger, one 4" x 4" piece pink felt or pink construction paper, one 4" x 4" piece of paper for pattern, "hair-colored" yarn, ribbon (enough for 2 hair bows or 1 bow tie), crayons or pieces of scrap felt for face, scissors, pencil, good glue, cloth suspension hanger

Procedure: Lay the coat hanger flat on table. Bend both wires of the hanger up at right angles on both sides about 3" from hook (sketch a). Squeeze the wires at each bend together so they are about 2" apart. Set the hanger on table with hook in the air. All surfaces of the bottom wire should be touching the table. If not, bend until they do. Draw face on pattern paper, cut out and trace on pink felt or paper. Cut out face. Color in features or cut them from scrap felt and glue on. Glue the head to the hook of the hanger (sketch b). Put the cloth suspension hanger on the back and hang in room or closet.

A cute bonnet holder can be made for the baby of the family by putting a baby face on the hanger and bending the coat hanger up 1" from each end.

Time required to make: 30 to 40 minutes

102

ROOSTER BOOKHOLDER

Materials: 1 wire coat hanger, one 2" styrofoam ball, 1 red pipe cleaner, ½ yellow pipe cleaner, 2 sequins of the same color, 2 straight pins

Procedure: Take the center of the hanger's cross wire and the hook and pull them away from each other to straighten and elongate the hanger (see sketch a). Lay the hanger on a flat surface and bend both wires up at right angles about 4" from the hook and bend up at right angles again about 5" from the first bend. The hanger should be U-shaped and the hook should face away from the center of the U (see sketch b). Push the styrofoam ball onto the hook. Accordion pleat the red pipe cleaner and insert into ball for comb (sketch c). Bend the yellow pipe cleaner and push into ball at the right place for beak. Pin 1 sequin on each side for eyes (sketch d). To use the bookholder, place books upright in the rooster's back.

Time required to make: 30 minutes

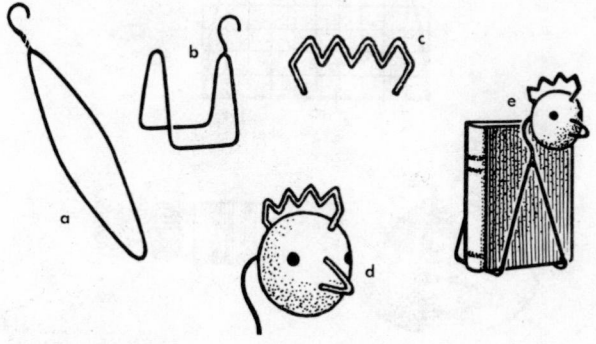

103

TELL THE STORY BEANIE

Materials: 5" x 5" pieces of felt in these colors: gold, black, white, red; four 27" white shoelaces, paper punch, 6 yards green yarn, 6" x 6" piece paper for pattern, cardboard 3" x 3", scissors

Procedure: Enlarge, trace and cut out pattern. (See sketch a.) Place on each piece of felt and cut out felt piece to match. If the child's head measures more than 20" around, enlarge cap by lacing it loosely. To make smaller, punch holes further in from edge. Punch 11 holes ¼" from edges down each side as in pattern. Lace sides together with shoelace starting at the bottom of triangle. Lace as you do shoes but cross the laces on the wrong side also. (See sketch b.) Do this to all sides. Colors going clockwise

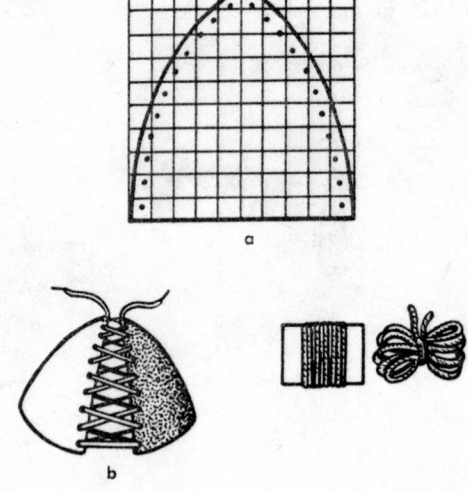

a

b

should be in this order: black, red, white, gold. Tie all the

104

shoelaces together where they meet on the inside of cap at the top.

Cut 6" off green yarn. Make pompon at top by wrapping green yarn around 3" cardboard until all used up. Slip off cardboard and tie in middle with 6" piece of yarn. Trim edges with scissors to make a fuzzy pompon. Tie pompon to top of cap with ends of 6" piece of yarn inserted through top holes. This cap can be used to tell the

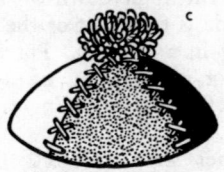

Wordless Book story. If you would like to trim the bottom edge of beanie, handstitch wide blue or black bias tape around it.

Time required to make: 40 to 60 minutes

HIKER'S PACK BAG

Materials: 1 printed grain sack or piece of heavy material such as denim 17" x 34"; 2 strips of 18" x 2" matching cloth; 2 curtain rings; a 48" length of heavy cord; 2 lengths of heavy cord 14" long; sewing materials; felt scraps for initials; scissors

Procedure: Cut a piece of grain sack or heavy cloth 17" x 34" and 2 strips 18" x 2". Fold 17" x 34" cloth in center and close 2 sides with French seams (sketch a). In center of 1 side cut a slit down 6" from the top and hem edges. This side is the front of the bag. Turn down top of bag and sew in a 1" hem. Put in the 48" drawstring and tie a knot in each end of string. Be sure to leave a few inches of string extending from both sides of opening (sketch a).

Fold each shoulder strap (18" x 2") right side out, so there will be a seam down the center. Sew securely (sketch b). Finished strap should be about ¾" wide. Sew 1 end of each strap to the back of bag, opposite the open-

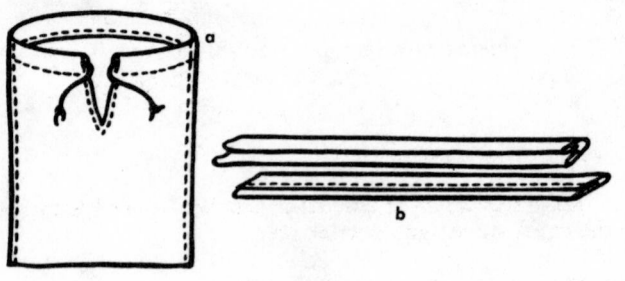

ing. Be careful not to sew into the draw cord. Sew curtain rings to the opposite ends of the straps. Tie a 14"

cord securely to each bottom corner of bag (see sketch c).
Put the other end of each cord through a curtain ring.
These straps can thus be adjusted to wearer's body
(sketch d).

Make monogram initials from felt (or cut out letters for
the entire name) and sew onto bag.

Time required to make: 2 to 4 hours

STILTS

Materials: 2 No. 2½-size tin cans with tops removed, 1 large nail, hammer, 8 ft. of heavy cord

Procedure: Remove the labels and wash cans. Punch 2 holes in opposite sides of the cans 1″ from closed end. Run heavy cord through holes so that ends comfortably reach hands when pupil is standing on cans (open end on ground). Tie firm knot inside can. To use, lift cord and can with each step.

Time required to make: 1 hour

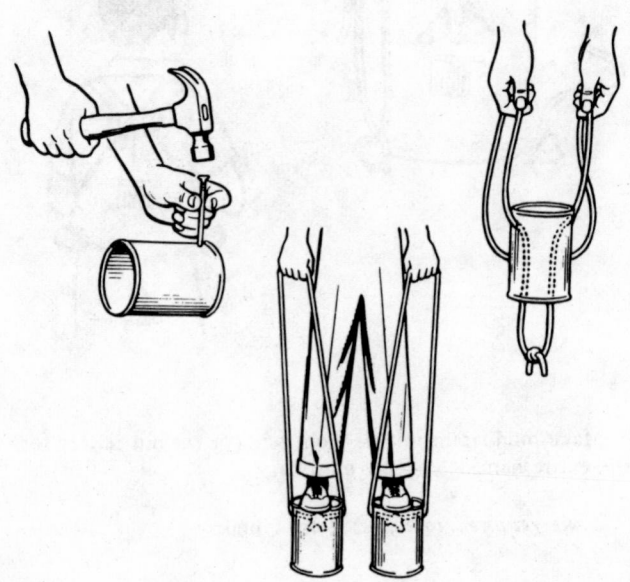

SAILOR'S DUFFEL BAG PURSE

Materials: Blue denim, 29" (width of material) by 10"; two 30" pieces of white rope; white textile paint; needle; thread

Procedure: Sew bag on wrong side across end and bottom. Make a 1" hem at top, leaving small openings on fold and seam sides of bag (sketch a). Draw or trace a nautical design in center of one right side of purse (sketch b). Then paint it and allow to dry, or applique white design on purse. Run each rope completely through the hem, each starting at the opening in opposite sides, and tie. Bag will be easy to close when handles are pulled away from each other.

Time required to make: 1 to 1½ hours

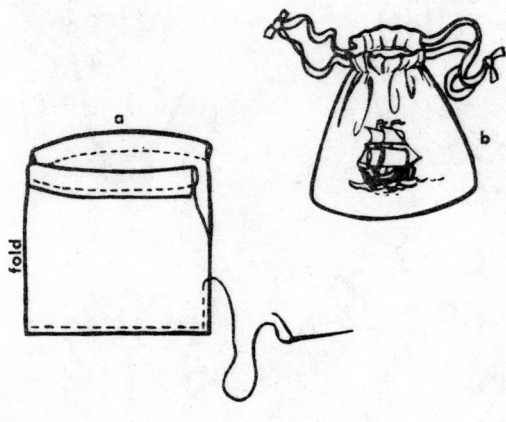

OCTOPUS PUPPET

Materials: 1 pair of cloth gloves; enough cotton to stuff 3 glove fingers; 4 pipe cleaners; 2 green thumbtacks; needle and thread; 1 rubber or Styrofoam ball 1½" in diameter; scissors

Procedure: Cut off cuff from left glove. Then cut the thumb and first two fingers from the glove as shown in sketch a. Slip middle finger of left glove over little finger of right glove and sew seams together carefully so that a finger still will fit into opening (see sketch b). Stuff other finger and thumb of left glove with cotton and sew to right glove (see sketch c). Cut another finger from left glove and stuff with cotton. Sew it fast between the thumb and forefinger on the right hand glove (sketch d).

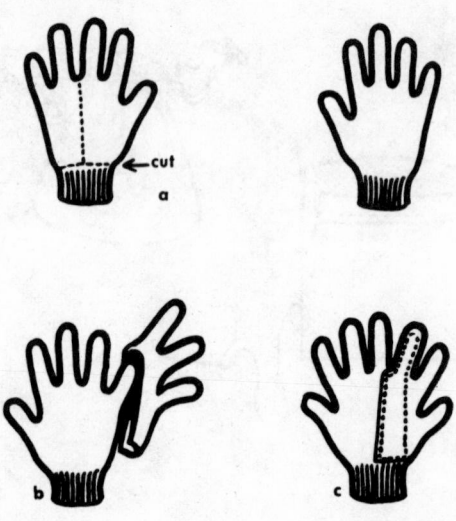

Cover ball with a portion of the left glove cuff and sew on right hand glove (see x on sketch e). Put 2 thumbtacks into ball for eyes.

Cut 4 pipe cleaners in half. Make a small loop in the end of each one (sketch f) and sew one securely to each finger tip. Curl pipe cleaners to look like tentacles. Now puppet is ready to wear (sketch g).

Time required to make: 1½ to 2 hours

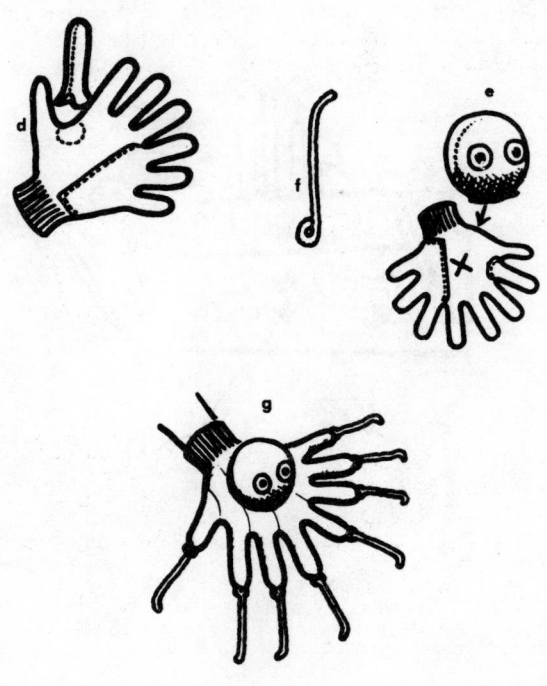

SHELF-N-COAT RACK

Materials: 1 apple crate, sandpaper, saw, nails, paint, brush, hammer, 3 small screw coat hooks

Procedure: Remove one side of crate. Saw ends in half diagonally. Sandpaper and paint. Nail to wall, screw in hooks. Shelf may be used for books or hats; hooks for coats.

Time required to make: 40 to 60 minutes

RECIPES

SOAPSUDS PAINT

>   1 cup any powder detergent
>   4 tbs. liquid starch

Mix detergent and starch and beat with a rotary beater until mixture is like frosting. If colored paint is desired, add powder paint or a drop of vegetable coloring.

Paint will last about one day so should be made on the day to be used. If the mixture becomes thick, add a little starch and beat it with a spoon. This recipe will provide paint for 8 to 10 children.

PASTE

>   1 cup sugar   1 qt. warm water
>   1 cup flour   1 tsp. powdered alum
>   Few drops oil of cloves

Mix dry ingredients in top of double boiler. Add water

slowly, stirring continuously. Cook until clear, and a little longer. Remove from fire, add oil of cloves, mixing thoroughly. Cool. Place in bottles or jars. Cover. Will keep for several months if carefully prepared. This recipe makes one quart.

SALT CLAY

Many interesting projects can be made from salt clay. It is easy to use, simple to prepare and washes off hands easily. Encourage originality. Trace the outline of object to be made on heavy cardboard. Draw in whatever design is desired beyond section where clay is to be applied. Shellac cardboard to keep it from absorbing the clay moisture. Mold clay on cardboard to show desired features. Allow time to dry—usually two days. Then if coloring was not mixed into clay, paint with water colors.

1 cup salt   1 cup water
2 cups flour   Vegetable coloring
Oil of cloves or oil of wintergreen, several drops

Mix salt and flour with water to consistency of heavy dough. Add oil of cloves or oil of wintergreen, mixing thoroughly. This acts as a preservative. Vegetable coloring can be kneaded into clay, or objects can be made first, then colored with water colors. This recipe makes about 12 pictures or small objects.

(To help the salt clay retain its shape better, make the dough a little more moist and then cook over low heat and stir until it is very thick.)

PAPIER-MACHE

Papier-mache craft can be very exciting and rewarding. You can make plaques, relief pictures, maps and models.

    1 newspaper (16 to 20 sheets)   Hot water
    1 tsp. powdered alum   1 pt. paste
              Optional—add starch or flour

Tear newspaper into small pieces and soak overnight in a pail of hot water. Shred between fingers until it is a pulpy mass. Pour off water or strain through a cloth. Add alum to paste and mix thoroughly with pulp. Add enough starch or flour, if desired, to make pulp the consistency of clay. Apply as desired to make a design on wood, cardboard, model, etc.

This recipe will make about 1/2 pail of papier-mache which is enough to make approximately 12 maps or flat objects. Allow two or three days for object to dry.

If you plan to cover an entire object, several layers of papier-mache may be needed. Paint with poster paints when dry. Shellac for permanence.

HINTS

PLASTER CASTING

Many lovely and useful articles can be made from plaster of Paris, molding plaster or patching plaster. All can be used the same way so shop around and purchase whichever is the cheapest.

Figurine, animal and motto molds are available for making objects to correlate with Bible lessons. Plaques and pins can be made practically expense free by all ages. The plaster also can be carved to make attractive pictures. Try these ways of using plaster and see what fun it is.

Nearly all plaster includes directions. For casting purposes, mix plaster with water until the consistency is that of a thick batter. Be very sparing when adding water! Remember, plaster hardens quickly and once it sets, it's set!

1. Molded plaster

One place where you may obtain figurine, animal or plaque molds is: Bersted's Hobby Craft, Inc., Monmouth, Illinois. Write for an illustrated catalog.

Wash molds in cold water and shake out. Inside should be damp. Prepare plaster and spoon it into mold. Squeeze out air bubbles and allow plaster to set (about 12 to 20 minutes). Gently peel mold—slowly—and trim off rough edges. Allow to dry completely, then paint with water colors or poster paints.

2. Plaster gifts

Obtain a supply of pictures, safety pins, adhesive tape, small fluted paper plates, milk cartons, colorless fingernail polish, hairpins, spoons, rubber furniture cups, Vaseline, plaster, bowl. (One two-pound package of plaster will make about 36 pins and about 24 plaques.)

Select the designs desired for pins or plaques from greeting cards. Prepare molds by cutting milk cartons down to within 1" of the bottom, or by greasing spoons, plates or rubber furniture cups lightly with Vaseline. Place picture or design face down in each mold and mark edge of mold where the top of pin or plaque is. Mix plaster with water until it is a thick pouring consistency. Pour into molds and set in sun.

To make a plaque, insert a hairpin in top of plaque for hanger when the plaster begins to "set." (Yarn or paper clips will also do. To make a pin, insert an open safety pin in plaster, being careful not to let the head fall in too deeply. Place a piece of adhesive tape across safety pin to prevent it from breaking out.

When plaster is hard, ease plaque or pin from mold. Cardboard and rubber molds are best since they are flexible. Use emery board to smooth off ends; cover with colorless fingernail polish. If twin pins are desired, fasten together with a length of gold or silver chain, available at the ten cent stores.

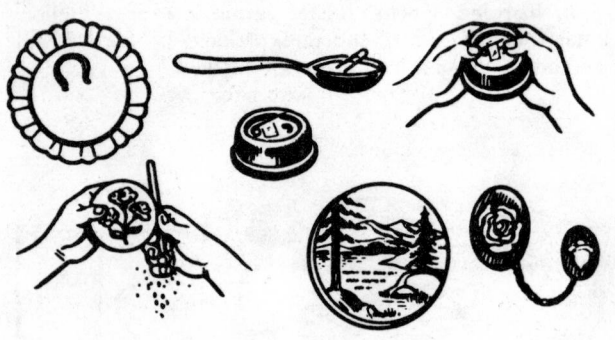

3. Carving in plaster

Use the above method for molding a plaque in a paper plate. While plaster is damp and still in mold, outline a design with an orange stick. As plaque dries, carve out the design in relief with orange stick or knife. Paint when dry.

HELPFUL HINTS for Patterns

There are patterns in this book to be prepared for use. You will also find designs elsewhere which you will want to use. The following hints will help you.

Tracing

Use tracing or tissue paper.

1. With small pieces of masking tape, fasten tracing paper lightly to page of book or on item to be traced. Trace around outline with sharp pencil.

2. To transfer tracing onto another surface, turn tracing paper over and cover back with pencil scribbles by using side of pencil lead.

3. With masking tape, anchor tracing on top of cloth or paper on which you wish to transfer design. Then go over lines of design with pencil. Remove tracing paper and design is transferred.

Enlarging and Reducing Patterns

To make the design twice as large:

1. On tracing paper, mark off every ½" lengthwise and crosswise. Draw in ½" squares with pencil and ruler.

2. Place this sheet over design and trace outline.

3. Make a copy sheet out of a second piece of tracing paper by ruling it off in 1" squares.

4. Study lines of design on the first tracing paper, then draw them in corresponding positions on the copy sheet.

To make the design half size:

1. Reverse method above.

2. Mark off first tracing sheet with ½" squares and copy sheet with ¼" squares.

When design is right size, transfer to material as instructed under "Tracing."

HOW TO CUT GLASS

Glass can be easily cut for use in making handcraft projects. Obtain a good glass cutter from a hardware store, a metal-edge ruler, a grease pencil, a piece of coarse grinding stone such as is used to sharpen tools.

Glass should be cut by adults for the younger child but teenagers can cut their own if they are properly shown how to do it. Care should be taken to avoid cuts and unplanned breakage.

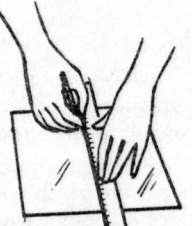

1. Measure and mark on glass with grease pencil the portions you wish to cut.

2. Hold a ruler firmly against glass on cutting line and press heavily with glass cutter as you pull or push it along the edge of the ruler.

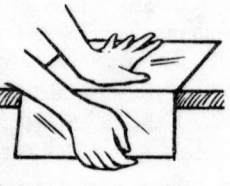

3. Place glass so the cutting line is on the edge of a table. Gently press the overhanging section until the glass breaks. Smooth all the edges gently with the grinding stone. For young children, the edges may be bound with Scotch tape to insure against accidental cuts.